McCLANE'S
ANGLING WORLD

SELECTED BOOKS BY A. J. McCLANE

The American Angler

*Spinning for Fresh and Salt Water Fish
of North America*

The Practical Fly Fisherman

McClane's New Standard Fishing Encyclopedia

Fishing with McClane

*McClane's Field Guide to Freshwater Fishes
of North America*

*McClane's Field Guide to Saltwater Fishes
of North America*

McClane's Secrets of Successful Fishing

McClane's Game Fish of North America
(with Keith Gardner)

Illustrations by
Gordon Allen

McCLANE'S
ANGLING WORLD

Al McClane's Greatest Adventures
Game Fishing Across America

A.J. McCLANE

T·T TRUMAN TALLEY BOOKS / E. P. DUTTON / NEW YORK

Portions of the material in this book appeared in different
form in *Field & Stream* and *Sports Afield.* Grateful acknowledgment
is given by the author to CBS Magazines and The Hearst
Corporation for their use.

Published in the United States by
Truman Talley Books • E. P. Dutton,
a division of New American Library,
2 Park Avenue, New York, N.Y. 10016.

Library of Congress Cataloging-in-Publication Data
McClane, A. J. (Albert Jules), 1922–
McClane's Angling world.
Includes index.
1. Fishing. 2. Fly fishing. I. Title.
II. Title: Angling world.
SH441.M43   1986   799.1   85-10357
ISBN: 0-525-24338-0

Published simultaneously in Canada by
Fitzhenry & Whiteside, Limited, Toronto

W

Designed by Mark O'Connor

10 9 8 7 6 5 4 3 2 1

First Edition

In memory of
Robert H. "Pete" Green
(1935–1985)

—whose career as a sportsman
was surpassed only
by his life as a man.

AUTHOR'S NOTE

I want to thank John Merwin, Executive Director of the American Museum of Fly Fishing in Manchester, Vermont, for his patience and expertise in selecting and editing the material contained in this book. John's remarkable talents as an author, editor, and angler are the binding to these pages, for which I am most grateful.

CONTENTS

McCLANE'S
ANGLING WORLD

1

FLOATERS ON THE FOAM

While rereading George LaBranche's *The Dry Fly and Fast Water* the other evening I recalled our only meeting in a Lexington Avenue spaghetti palace, when the cologne-splashed dandy held a séance on the history of American angling. Although none of my marinara-stained notes ever reached print, simply because anything the man said was an epic in itself, it was apparent that both his treatise (published in 1914) and subsequently *The Salmon and the Dry Fly* (released ten years later) were pioneer works. Bear in mind that LaBranche was touting a 3½-ounce fly rod and extolling the virtues of precision and delicacy in casting before Henry built the first Model A Ford.

1

LaBranche was eighty years old when we broke bread, yet he described every important detail of any stream I could namedrop—even my boyhood favorite, Basket Brook, which hardly rated as a memorable watercourse, although Ray Bergman fished it from time to time, and, to me at least, *his* boots sanctified its currents. Turn-of-the-century dry-fly fishing was focused on slow water over rising trout, but LaBranche advised anglers to wade into tumbling streams and cast on "anything short of a perpendicular waterfall." This now commonplace technique, he said, was considered heresy and "invited the wrath of gods upon my head," an Elizabethan phrase which befitted a man in high collar and Harris tweeds who could twirl linguini around his fork with the expertise of Rome's Alfredo.

It's impossible to reduce any kind of angling to a set of rules, but there are certain things about fast-water fishing that, if kept in mind, will make catching trout a little easier. To begin with, I would suggest the lightest possible tackle—not necessarily a midge rod but one designed for a 4-weight line. Short casts, whether upstream or down, are far more effective than a long line dragging over broken currents, and the heavier the taper the quicker it will pull a fly under. Three-diameter lines that are calibered like well-fed boa constrictors will neither float nor fish properly. Furthermore, there usually isn't enough distance involved in fast-water fishing to get the belly portion out of the guides. A double taper is much superior.

For ultimate ease in the controlled float of a dry fly I would recommend a 3-weight line, which weighs just 100 grains. I realize it doesn't always appear in catalogs, but a 3-weight size is made by one of our leading line manufacturers and can be ordered by your dealer. The 3-weight reaches .030 inch at the point, which is the smallest diameter a braid can be bonded in modern plastics while still retaining enough weight for a good turnover. Many fly lines run from .037 to .040 inch at the point, which is not insignificant. A thick line point has a number of disadvantages: its greater diameter has more water resistance and is less flexible, thereby creating drag almost instantly; it requires the use of extra-heavy leader butts that add rigidity to the terminal end where free movement is required. Bear in mind that in speaking of the line "point" we are considering the first 2 feet of a fly line and at least part of the front taper. For my fishing, the 10 feet nearest the trout must not weigh more than 30 grains and the diameter should run from .030 to no more than .040 at the 10-foot mark. The first 30 feet (which is the portion that counts in our line-weighing system) must not exceed 120 grains. This more or less approximates a DT4 size. At normal casting distances a 30-foot length of light fly line guarantees lifelike presentation of the fly.

The next material requirement, an air-resistant fly, is seemingly a contradiction to everything we seek of our tackle, as the theorem reads that anything we do to overcome air resistance will increase the length of a cast. However, the rule is a relative one, and doesn't apply to presentation of the fly. Remember that the cast is gone, the line has straightened in the air, and the leader is making its dying gasp. Until this instant, the size or type of dry fly (within normal limits) had no influence on the velocity or momentum of the cast. Now, in harmony with line point and leader, the fly may fall in a variety of ways. A fly dressed on a heavy hook or tied with short, sparse hackles will hit the surface hard and begin dragging rather quickly. A spider-type fly with its long hackles and light wire hook, on the other hand, has the flight characteristics of a dandelion seed and can skim over broken currents without being pulled under.

In LaBranche's day the Fanwing Royal Coachman was a "must" on U.S. trout waters because of its air resistance and ability to float high on the surface. The trouble with a Fanwing is that it twists and weakens the leader tippet, and after one toothy trout has mauled the feathers it loses its cocky stance. A spider, however, is virtually impossible to present badly or fish poorly over fast water. A proper spider is made from spade hackle, the wide hackle found on a rooster's throat. Sometimes on a gamecock skin you'll find saddle hackles that are perfect for making spiders; as a rule, however, they are a bit too short. The hooks I like best are #14 and #16 short shanks of very light wire. Spiders will not spin or twist a light leader, and although they have little more air resistance than orthodox dry flies, once the cast is checked they execute a slow, deliberate flight to the surface. Furthermore, the spider is less apt to drag on the water, because a pull on the line will send the fly hopping out of trouble. Remember, this fly cocks on the tips of its long hackles and tail with the hook well above the surface. It can even be cast directly downstream and purposely dragged against the current; if your line is floating high, the spider will simply walk upstream.

Bivisibles and flies dressed with clipped hair bodies

and wings are also buoyant and virtually all standard patterns tied with slightly oversize hackles are easier to float than standard ties. One of our late and fabled Catskill fly makers, whose floaters were renowned, used #11, #13, and #15 hooks for what appeared to be #10, #12, and #14 dressings. Ordinarily, fast-water trout are not too critical as far as pattern is concerned. They will grab what an erratic fortune serves them. But sometimes the fly size can make a considerable difference. If you move a fish and he refuses the pattern, try a smaller size. There is little time for the trout to scrutinize and select, yet he is often dubious of an insect that is larger than it ought to be.

There are two things you might keep in mind that deviate from the norm. One is that a trout will occasionally accept a drowned dry fly in swift water, and it's best to fish a cast out rather than snatch line in the air to make a new cast. No doubt the fish finds it perfectly natural to see an insect abruptly sucked down in the current. The other thing is that repetitive casting, which is a bugbear on a limpid surface, will often raise fish in the bubbly. I suspect that a trout's vision can be impaired by the current, and those acrobatic strikes we get in swift water when the fish jumps over the fly are triggered by the trout's need to locate his target on a frothy surface. From below the fly is frequently a shadow, half formed and half lost in the fish's vision.

While I was standing with Tom McNally at the edge of the highway that parallels Montana's turbulent Gallatin River, a truck driver pulled his rig into an adjacent parking spot. He ambled over to bum a smoke and pass the time.

"No sense in fishing the river here," he announced.

"Why?" McNally asked.

"When trout get in fast water like that they're too busy swimming to eat."

Our informant supplied other bits of angling wisdom,

including a 50-mile drive back to Bozeman to find properly slow water in which trout joyously feed. Although the Gallatin has never been an outstanding fish-producer in my experience, if you know the spots above Gateway, an afternoon's outing can provide a lot of fun with foot-long rainbows and the occasional larger brown. Our biggest fish that day was a 15-incher who bounced out of a run of whitewater that defied wading.

Individually, trout always seek a position in the river where they can face the current with a minimum of effort. The actual lair may be nothing more than a depression in the stream bottom where the full force of the current has been deflected upward by some rocks—or behind a log, an undercut, or in the pocket formed by a large boulder that splits the current. A rapid flow of water brings a great deal of food to the trout who dashes from the protected place to grab his meal "in flight," so to speak. This is particularly hard on hatchery stock who do not have the stamina necessary for life in fast water, nor the ability to distinguish between food objects and bits of surface drift such as twigs or weed. A wild trout, on the other hand, becomes very adept at nailing a tiny fly as it skims along the bubbly surface, and he is more discriminating; we often see a big rainbow boil behind an artificial in the water so swift that one can't help but admire his dexterity and wit. The "screen" of surface turbulence permits us to work much closer to the fish without spooking him, but the ground rules of artful fly casting must be observed nevertheless.

There has never been any doubt in my mind that downstream dry-fly fishing is often more productive in fast water than casting upstream. However, it's tactically essential to learn both techniques, and these can only be debated one at a time. In rivers with an abundance of large protruding boulders, for example, such as the upper Connecticut in New Hampshire or the Gallatin, trout hold on the "blind side" to a downstream caster. This severely limits the number of fish you can cover without losing control of the line and the swim of the fly. I am talking about pocket water as opposed to long, freckly riffles with submerged rocks that can be worked handily in any direction.

Pockets are, in effect, a series of miniature pools complicated by the existence of swift currents surrounding them; to extract the best fish from each one you have to be accurate and achieve drag-free floats. What makes a pocket awkward to cover in a downstream direction is that trout lie in a relatively narrow area which usually contains a small back eddy, a dead spot, and then an accelerating point that boils up into a slick. Drag is an absolute certainty. But the angler who faces upstream can delay it for precious seconds.

Sometimes a fish will come indecisively, tugging but not taking hold, or rolling over the fly, but most strikes are solid, which inevitably accounts for a great number of broken tippets in fast water. A reflexive strike is necessary, but if it's uncontrolled, it's fatal. Nevertheless, there's nothing to be gained in using heavy tackle. If anything, pocket fishing requires complete mastery of the short cast.

Getting down to the nitty-gritty, how you approach the fish determines to a large extent how the fly will be presented. Fast, bouldery water is seldom easy to negotiate; long before lunch even a daily jogger can get rubbery-legged from leaning against the flow. An experienced angler examines each run not only with an eye to potential hot spots, but with his own progress in mind. It may be necessary to pass up two or three pockets because they don't fit into the checkerboard moves you'll have to make in order to keep your feet. I try to sight along a string of pockets that permit my taking advantage of the slower currents, first by fishing one, and then by wading one to fish the next. As a rule, this requires only a few short steps through fast water at the head of one pocket in order to reach the tail of the one above.

On small streams you may not need to wade, but to hold a tactical advantage always try to cast from a position where your line is not caught in an accelerating current. This is most difficult on mountain streams with a steep gradient, where the water tumbles as though spilling down a flight of stairs, but it can be overcome to a large extent by completing each cast in the air. The rod must be checked so the fly and leader come to the surface *before* the line, or at least simultaneously with it. If the line falls first, as it often does, it will be swept back with the flow and commence dragging before the fly is on target. Tackle does make a difference in this game.

When using my 2¾-ounce rod and 100- to 120-grain double-taper line and a balanced leader, I can generally place the fly on the surface with, or sometimes before, the line point. Much depends on the size of the fly and wind conditions. However, with my 8½-foot rod and 160- to 165-grain weight-forward line, I rarely get a "fly-first" presentation, and only occasionally put the leader down simultaneously with the line point. This heavier rod is a real weapon on big streams where long casts are necessary, but it's a handicap if I have to please a fussy trout underfoot. The point is that no single outfit can do all jobs, and the more weight you eliminate, the faster you'll shoot from the hip.

Leader design and diameter are important. If out of balance, the leader will arrive on the water a critical second after the line has started floating quickly back to your feet. Personally, I use the longest leader that will cast efficiently at short ranges, which usually works out to 10 to 12 feet. The longer the leader, the longer you can delay drag. In addition, it allows the fly to twist and turn like a natural insect. Although short casts and long leaders may sound incompatible, this is not true when the leader is correctly balanced. A good leader can be cast in a perfect turnover with your bare hand. Obviously, it's even easier to straighten it with a few feet of line extended from a rod tip. A balanced leader consists of 60 percent heavy diameters, 20 percent gradation, and 20 percent tippet. In other words, the butt section should be the longest part of a leader of any given length. This is contrary to the common commercial practice of making short butts, or sections of equal length.

Also, the fly size must be proportionate to the tippet diameter. With the wrong tippet, a tiny #20 midge can be as difficult to lay down as an 8/0 salmon fly. Because of its minuscule dressing, the midge offers no air resistance and merely goes along with the leader for a free ride. For this reason, long, fine tippets are necessary, since they are air-resistant in themselves. In other words, they absorb that final flea power at the turnover and settle down easily. The tippet length and diameter for proper midge fishing would collapse if you were to use it with #10 dry flies. Conversely, the idea of improving your presentation with a #10 by using an extra-fine tippet is not practical. The larger fly has considerable air resistance in itself, and, if the tippet is too fine, it will delay the turnover, or fall in a tangled heap. It works both ways.

Again, there are no handy rules to follow but it's possible to analyze your presentation by studying the flow of line and leader in the turnover. Does the leader suddenly flop back on the line on a forward cast and fold up on the back cast? If so, you may need a heavier and longer butt section. Does the leader drag behind the outgoing line and gradually fall back as the cast straightens out? If so, it is probably too light for its length. There are many symptoms that can be diagnosed and corrected before you begin fishing—and this checkup is more important than choosing the right fly.

Where dry-fly fishing is concerned, much of what we believe to be success due to changing to a killing pattern is in reality success due to finally tying on a fly that balances with the leader tippet and line point. A bushy bivisible, even though it's tied on, say, a #14 hook, will not deliver in the same fashion as a sparsely dressed pattern such as the Cahill, even though the hook size may be the same. While the effect is not felt with a heavy leader, it will make all the difference in the world with the light tippet a #14 hook requires. This is an obvious point to old-timers but it is not readily understood among the vast majority of beginners.

George LaBranche was by all accounts an exceptional caster (according to the venerable *Fishing Gazette,* which commented on his skill during a visit to Britain's chalk-streams: "His flies go where he wishes them to go and act as he directs them when they get there"), and, typically, the maestro described fast-water fly fishing in terms of music: "The fly could be allowed to float on the water for a certain length of notes, withdrawn, and the line straightened out and cast again, all to musical measure and cadence."

Using the proper instruments, that's about as good a description as any.

Clinic

Although trout thrive in fast water, individually they station themselves at the current interface, where the flow slackens and little energy is required to hold their positions. The slick water behind an emergent rock, for example, is really a miniature pool where a fish can hold effortlessly yet dart left or right for any insect borne by adjacent swift currents. The trout will also hold in that cushion of water that forms over or behind submerged rocks, so even where the stream is uniformly fast and broken you can find slick spots and expect surface rises. The swift flow of a riffle into an undercut bank, especially where a stream makes a bend, is an ideal feeding location as drifting foods concentrate here and the trout hold near bottom where the current has dissipated. Even in a straight run, where the flow is along a deep bank, trout will hold in pockets just a foot or two out of the fast water; this requires working your fly as close to the bank as possible. Logs and downed trees lying in the stream, whether in deep or shallow water, not only break the stream flow but provide excellent cover. Here again, feeding fish will hold in the current interface at the very edge of the main flow.

2

A FISH OF FABLE

During the thirty years that I was charged with world record keeping, no species of fish created more migraines than the northern pike. Fortunately, I did not have to referee the last donnybrook over a 62½-pound pike taken in Lake Bieler (Bieler See), Switzerland, a perfectly authentic specimen, but alas, not destined for immortality in the record book. After the details were sorted out by that Swiss angling journal *Petri Heil* and the German angling magazine *Blinker,* it was discovered that the monster had been legally netted by commercial fishermen, then sold alive to the angler who "caught" it elsewhere. Swiss restaurants are not fond of big pike, so the subsequent capture by the same man of three more, each weighing over 40 pounds, is, if nothing else, testimony to the productivity of Lake Bieler.

That alpine angler was an amateur in the art of deception. Buying a record pike is easy, but building one requires talent. The classic hoax occurred in 1497 when a pike of 350 pounds was "caught" in Germany. The skeleton of this 19-foot Gothic Jaws was long displayed in the cathedral of Mannheim—perhaps an atheistic symbol to strike down at Sunday sermons. The rubbery hand of a curator had done a creditable job in the sectional reconstruction of Lord knows how many fish bones, deluding enough people to keep the legend alive for generations.

Prevarication sticks to the pike like slime to its skin. Torpedo-shaped, duck-billed, poker-faced, with a canine-toothed mouth that is a dental nightmare, this 20-million-year-old survivor of an extinct forebear, *Esox lepidotus* (the modern northern is *Esox lucius*), inspires the makers of fables. For centuries it was believed that pike swallowed small boys, swans, even mules.

Yet behind all this is a noble gamefish slowly swimming into the dawn of a new era.

Just two decades ago the fisheries resources in Canada were close to disaster. Squadrons of bush planes were exploiting remote waters, bag limits were too generous, and big female breeders were being killed like there was no tomorrow.

The decimation of 10- to 40-year-old stocks of gamefish was then commonplace, and our northern pike—alias the hammerhandle, snake, jackfish, shovelnose, chukwuk, and slinker—were often killed in obscene numbers for no reason except to hang them at the dock for a collective photo, where they looked like a gang of pop-eyed rustlers swinging in the wind over Boot Hill.

It was a Swedish clergyman, Hans Hederstrom, who, in

1759, doubting the tale of the 262-year-old Mannheim pike, observed that fish vertebrae are imprinted with concentric rings, similar to the annuli found in tree trunks; from these vertebrae he determined growth rates for pike and other species that are comparable to modern scientific estimates. Although Hederstrom was shedding light in dark corners, the science of ichthyology did not move on winged sandals. A century and a half passed before Sweden awarded him a gold medal for his *Observations on the Age of Fishes.*

By 1932 it was established (in a study by D. W. Rawson on Waskesiu Lake in Saskatchewan) that a wilderness pike population can be seriously depleted by angling pressure. Since it takes 10 to 12 years for a female pike to grow to 25 pounds in favorable conditions (males seldom exceed 10 pounds), the rapid recruitment of trophy fish is about as logical as W. C. Fields attending an AA meeting.

In the arctic latitude of Great Bear Lake, a 12-year-old pike would weigh only about 8 pounds, as compared to an 8-year-old pike weighing from 35 to 50½ pounds in the temperate limestone lakes of Ireland. In the slow-growth habitats of Canada and Alaska, where nature compensates with longer life spans of 18 to 20 years, pike exist in a very fragile oligotrophic environment. What has become significant in the north country is a one-fish limit imposed by some camp operators and politely suggested by others.

This pivotal "trophy only" concept—not new to United States trout waters—has spread to camps such as Mike Dyste's lodge at Little Churchill, Brian McIntosh's camp at Sickle Lake, Jerry Bricker's Frontier Lodge, and Brabant's Lodge on Great Slave Lake and various other locations where conservation is paramount.

Although the pike has long been identified with flashing spoons and wiggling plugs, there is a new coterie of fly fishermen who find the waterwolf a challenging adversary. The feather game is an old one, dating back in print to H. Cholmondeley Pennel (*The Book of the Pike,* 1865), but its popularity has only boomed in the last decade. Dr. Elmer Rusten of Plymouth, Minnesota, who has been fishing northerns for thirty-five seasons, now operates solely with the fly and has run up a record number of releases with more than 40 trophy pike to his credit—the biggest at 25 pounds.

Undeniably, pike action can be fast and furious. In classic piscine style, they are not acrobatic. I hooked several fish in Reed Lake, Manitoba, that came out of the water as if shot from a cannon; yet later, on the same trip fishing the shallow backwaters of the Winnipeg River, I took scores of pike and not one became airborne.

Invariably, northerns surge, splash, head-shake, run in circles, and raise hell at boatside—quick to get under the hull and wrap your line around the outboard. As a grand finale they often do the Red Baron's victory roll and get trussed in the leader like a Christmas turkey. Even the most jaded angler, though, will experience heart stoppers because pike don't rise to a fly with a dainty sip. They charge full speed with a spine-tingling wake, sometimes nailing the feathers under your rod tip. I once had a pike miss my streamer and land in our skiff—smack in the lunch basket. At times it would seem that pike have as much fun as their anglers.

When the snow came down in a whirling veil that last day in September, all we had left in our larder was a bag of beans, some onions, a slab of bacon, and a bottle of bourbon. Naturally, the plane that was due didn't show up. My wife and I were staying in a cabin at Barney Lamm's old out-camp while I located brook trout spawning areas in Gods River for Bert Kooyman, director of fisheries in Manitoba. Patti and I had a snowball fight that morning to celebrate her birthday, then went down to the rapids, our whitefish hot spot, and caught nothing.

Our next surefire spot was a shoal in the lake. We were using spinning tackle with ¼-ounce wobbling spoons, and here we boated a pair of pike of about 4 pounds each—just the right size for eating. I wanted to head for the stove and the bourbon but Patti insisted on making one more cast. About ten throws later she tied into a brute that came out of the water in slow motion, a long arcing leap that looked eerie in the falling snow. I expected the pike, on 6-pound-test and minus a leader, to break off instantly. For the next twenty minutes we covered a lot of Gods acres with the fish porpoising and head-shaking in long runs.

I never saw a pike fight so frantically, and no wonder: It was lassoed. A couple of turns of monofilament were looped around its caudal peduncle just above the tail and secured fast by the little treble which was embedded in its skin. The fish was easily 16 to 18 pounds, too big for the pan, but it provided an epic birthday performance.

You don't need a Latin vocabulary to understand a pike's menu: fish, tadpoles, frogs, snakes, leeches, ducklings, mice, muskrats—just about anything that will fit in its mouth, including other pike. It is capable of ingesting fish from one-third to one-half its own length. This gastronomic debauchery would suggest that almost anything you throw into the water will take pike. In the bush-camp littoral this is often so, but in heavily fished regions they become sophisticated at an early age.

For a long time I was under the impression that saltwater bucktails, the kind we use for tarpon and striped bass, were ideal for pike. They worked fine in the boondocks where hungry fish are stacked like cordwood, but splashy refusals in civilized Wisconsin and Ontario lakes occurred too often.

I eventually learned that northerns respond quickly to long flies that snake and flutter through the water. Bucktail doesn't provide that erratic action. There is a comparison here with the barracuda, who has a similar taste in artificials; old razormouth will gobble an undulating surgical-tube lure after spurning a live pilchard.

One of my most effective flies for pike is the New Zealand Bunny. The Bunny is made from a long strip of rabbit hide with fur intact. The strip is tied palmer-style on the hook shank with a wiggly tail section extending past the bend. I suppose you could use muskrat, fox, or any other fur.

My other favorite is the McNally Magnum. Tom McNally, outdoor editor of the *Chicago Tribune* and long-time exponent of pike on the fly, has scored releases in the thousands, with his biggest at 26 pounds. His pattern is a red and yellow streamer, with a 5- to 7-inch-long saddle hackle wing tied on 1/0 to 5/0 short-shank hooks. The Magnum is surprisingly easy to cast and the wing has a

lively flutter, so much so that I've often taken pike while the fly was slowly sinking before the retrieve.

To prevent the pike's teeth from cutting the fly off, it's important to use a 12-inch shock tippet of 20- to 30-pound-test *hard* nylon. This can be joined to your regular leader tippet with a surgeon's knot. The fly should be tied to the shock tippet with a Homer Rhode or similar loop knot to allow it to swing freely. Any knot that jams against the hook eye will hold the fly rigid in the water when heavy tippets are used. Tying a loop may take a little more time, but it makes a world of difference in fly action.

I've often wondered what the maximum size of a pike might be. Throughout Europe, in pubs, restaurants, country inns, and castles, you can find huge pike with mouths agape mounted in glass cases—fish running into the fat 50s. So in Ireland I hired a gillie who had rheumatism, which required my rowing his clinker-built wooden skiff for two days in a howling wind on Lough Mask. I caught one pike, hardly bigger than the spoon, and fell into total exhaustion. Then I tried the Baltic shores of Sweden. I caught plenty of small pike here, but a pair of trumpeter swans nearly beat my brains out when I waded near their nest. In Bavaria I was delivered to the area of a nude bathing beach, which my host, with elaborate conviction, insisted was the best spot on the lake. I couldn't disagree, but all we caught was eyestrain.

These and other painful memories aside, we know the Bieler See monster was 62½ pounds, and there is evidence that a 72-pound pike was taken in Loch Ken, Scotland, back in 1788. The skull of the latter was preserved in Kenmure Castle and examined by the eminent biologist Dr. Tate Regan in 1910. The cranium was 9 inches in width with a spread of 6 inches across jaws bearing inch-long canine teeth. Anatomically, these proportions suggest that the Kenmure pike was no fable. Typical of pike legends, the skull disappeared, but was recovered in 1952, evidently banished by the royal family to a Kenmure outhouse. Growing conditions in many European lakes make such a weight plausible. In the subalpine waters of Germany, for example, even brown trout reach prodigious weights—for instance, a 55-pound brown from the Walchensee and a 60-pound, 9-ounce brown from the Königsee in 1976. These submarines were netted by hatchery personnel for spawn taking.

There are those who believe that one day a great pike bigger than the Bieler See captive will fall victim to her own appetite—a villainous slap at a spoon and old *Esox* will find immortality. With 20 million years of survival, don't bet on it.

Clinic

Action is the keynote in taking pike on the fly. Taking into account the large sizes required to attract these toothy predators, I consider the Homer Rhode loop knot a real plus when rigging my terminal tackle. Unlike any of the jams or knots that are cinched against the hook eye, a loop allows the fly to swing freely. Many small plugs and jigs also work better in the water when attached with a loop. And unlike the popular Duncan loop or hangman's noose, which slips down against the eye when a fish is hooked, theoretically providing greater security, the Homer Rhode remains in place. Personally, I've never had any trouble with the latter when using heavy-shock-tippet material of hard monofilament, even with tarpon in the 100-pound class. The Homer Rhode is easy to tie, and, when it's finally formed, I pull it tight with a pair of pliers. I have taken a few Saint Lawrence muskellunge while pike fishing, and I suspect that these cunning members of the genus *Esox* are also stimulated by the fluttering fly action that a loop permits. The late Homer Rhode, incidentally, was a master saltwater fisherman, a pioneer in taking marlin and sailfish on the fly.

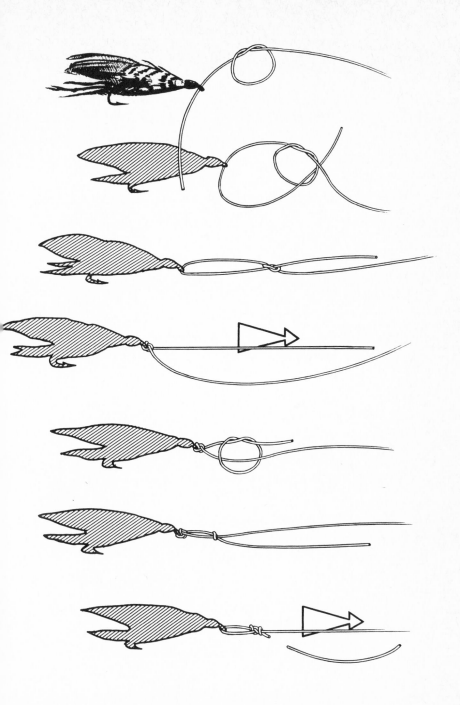

Homer Rhode loop knot

3

A RED BADGE OF COURAGE

Haya! Haya! Come up again Swimmer . . .
Welcome Supernatural One, you Long-
Life-Maker for you come to set me right
again as is always done by you.
—FROM THE KWAKIUTL INDIAN PRAYERS
TO SALMON AND STEELHEAD

They come from the sea with the first fall rains; they come
with the snows and they come when the earth smells green.
Over the bars and past the winkled half-tide rocks where
sea perch and rust-colored dabs drift across their secret
paths in the kelp, they come in creeping, hesitant runs,
then halting as though drugged by an osmotic change from

years in distant deeps to that now thin liquid forming an unlit street. There are wraiths to be avoided—a seal, an otter, or simply the shadows of gulls. And in the precise rhythm born with time, as the tide swells in their favor, the silver phalanx runs boldly forward again to begin a journey that may last hundreds of miles, where the hen will violently tail her natal stones to hide golden pearls of spawn before she is spent and dark with winter's chill. Another color emerges too. The bright armor forged in the Pacific has long given way to a growing lateral band—the red badge of courage that is the rainbow trout's. The male steelhead is newly toothed in grotesque jaws, a fierce visage, a primitive war mask for the strength he no longer enjoys. But then the rainbow is a fish of many faces, and while we may forever debate the proposition, it has only one peer as a freshwater gamefish—the Atlantic salmon.

I caught my first steelhead within a short cast of Roderick L. Haig-Brown's home on the Campbell River in British Columbia—which is like a sinner in sackcloth taking his vows with the Dalai Lama. My Eastern boyhood experience with wild rainbow trout was limited, as there were few streams with reproducing populations in the Catskills: Callicoon Creek and the Esopus held river-born fish, and I occasionally caught a few big ones from the Delaware, which in those days was primarily a smallmouth bass stream. The only large migrations of rainbows were in the Finger Lakes region, where my career reached its nadir on a trip to Catherine Creek. Anglers stood shoulder-to-shoulder like Gary Cooper's beady-eyed Bengal Lancers facing the Dervishes. One spawner was often hooked by two or three rods simultaneously, lured by frozen lumps of petroleum jelly colored with Mercurochrome, hanks of red yarn, red golf tees, and other baits too bizarre to list. Except for heated debates about who caught the fish, it was as exciting as extracting sardines from a can.

A lot of gravel has rolled underfoot since then. I remember that glorious summer-run 10-pounder I took on a dry fly while fishing with Pop Morris at the old Blue Creek Camp on the Klamath in California. Pop was an over-seventy-year-old Ichabod Crane who danced on algae-slick boulders with impunity. He tied all his flies upside down, convinced that steelhead hooked in the roof of the mouth were inspired to greater heights. And there was Johnny Walatka's original tent camp on the Brooks River in Alaska, where I took Patti on our honeymoon in 1952 to catch her first 30-inch rainbow—which she carefully released. I can still see the tundra and wolf willows, the ptarmigan bursting from peavines, and still hear the methodical slap of ice-coated fly line against water in the silent world of snow. For two chilling weeks we shared one sleeping bag and a meager supply of sour mash; the urban carnality of Niagara Falls wouldn't offer much more than walleye fishing, however, which only proves the backwardness of travel agents. Although I never pursued rainbow trout with the dedication that millionaire *New York Herald* publisher James Gordon Bennett invested in his search for the perfect mutton chop (in less violent moments he was known to throw an offending chop onto the floor, and in a display of passion he bought Ciro's of Monte Carlo, a restaurant that served properly aged double-rib Southdowns, so he could dine without risk whenever he was in town), I did know that somewhere there was often one river, or one lake, that produced exceptional rainbows— not always bigger, but somehow the best of the breed.

In his scholarly work *Steelhead Fly Fishing and Flies,* which is literally drenched with data and lore, and which, together with his earlier volume *Steelhead Trout,* comprises more than you need to know about the anadromous rainbow, author Trey Combs observes that Dean River steelhead are the strongest of all, rivaled only by the fish of the

Thompson River. This long-held angling belief was confirmed by British Columbia fishery biologists, who placed various races of steelhead in tanks and subjected the trout to currents of sustained velocities—running them on an aquatic treadmill, so to speak. The Dean and Thompson river trout proved to have as much as four times the stamina of steelhead from other watersheds. Although I haven't fished either stream since the 1950s (we went safari-style to the lower Dean in a Ford trimotor on floats), my recollection is that both produced real "tackle busters," as compared to many rivers where the trout perform nobly but without the speed and acrobatics of the Dean and Thompson strains.

In common with other salmonids, particularly the Atlantic salmon, various racial stocks of rainbow differ in their fighting ability. Any opinion as to which is the better gamefish must take into account a number of factors, and size is usually the first thing that comes to mind.

One might expect that the bigger the fish the greater its resistance, but in my experience that just isn't true. The rainbow I will never forget was a 16¾-pounder I took from Michigan's Au Sable River in October 1971 while fishing with Paul Harvey. I have taken heavier fish elsewhere, but never one that was almost continuously airborne—leaping, cartwheeling, doing bellywhoppers like a kid on a Flexible Flyer. This may seem like hyperbole, but it actually churned across the surface in the posture of a greyhounding marlin. This deep-bodied 32-inch trout, a record for the Au Sable, was canonized by a local taxidermist and now hangs on its walnut plaque in the Lakewood Shores bar at Oscoda—in tribute to its demise. I sank in over my wader tops and finally sat down in a frigid backwater while slowly steering that fish into my lap. After twenty-five minutes of acrobatics, it was as dead as the proverbial doornail. Not even in the salad days of Peru's Lake Titicaca, when 16- to

18-pound fish were par for the course and the daily score-
card might include a 27-, 28-, or even a 30-pounder (with
the lake record at 34 pounds), did any of these fish provide
more than a competent performance—one, maybe two
jumps, then a sullen tug-of-war, *thump, thump, thump,* like
a gut-busting grouper trying to find a hole in the coral. It
didn't matter whether the trout were caught in the lake or
its tributary streams. But on a still morning at 14,000 feet,
when a giant rainbow rolls out of crystalline water and
shatters the mirrored surface into a hundred images of
itself, well, the overture was better than the opera and
that's often what angling is all about.

One of the "hottest" inland rainbow fisheries today is
the Bow River in Alberta. The strain of trout found there
seldom grows into double-digit figures, but these fish have
more bounce to the ounce. The 4- and 5-pounders wheel
into the current and get into your backing like bonefish,
and everybody who visits the stream is impressed by their
stamina. As much as I delight in catching rainbows in the
Yellowstone and Madison, those fish just aren't in the same
league.

When we speak of a strain or race of trout, it may
encompass a subspecies; and while the latter term is useful
to designate salmonids of a particular watershed, it has
little meaning in making taxonomic distinctions. Many
rainbow populations have been isolated for untold thousands of years, and some morphological separation has
inevitably occurred. When Jordan and Evermann were
cataloging our trout in 1902 (*American Food and Game Fishes*),
it was believed that a number of rainbow subspecies, even
distinct species, existed. The major differences described
other than coloration and spotting were in the scale
counts. Some thirty years later, however, Dr. Charles M.
Mottley discovered that these meristics in the rainbow
were a reflection of existing environmental conditions dur-

ing the early development of the fish. For example, the
progeny of rainbows from Kootenay Lake, British Columbia, showed scale counts that varied according to the
time of egg deposition. The difference was related to water
temperature. Fish resulting from a spawn that occurred
late in the run and at a higher temperature varied from the
population as a whole, with the number of scale rows decreasing. An even greater change was induced by rearing
fish at a higher temperature in a hatchery, with the number
of scale rows decreasing further as the temperature in-

creased. Today, sophisticated phylogenetic studies are based on the amino acid sequence of protein molecules and the relationship between the chromosomes of different genotypes.

As with the brook trout, a century of domestication—especially in the midwestern and eastern United States—had a tremendous impact on the rainbow, diluting the "genetic message" in some cases and delivering a new version in others. The domestic Whitney strain, for example, was derived from McCloud River stock at the turn of the century and was apparently crossed at various times with steelhead from the Eel River and Lahontan cutthroat from Lake Tahoe—a rather sporty heritage. Drawing a composite picture of the rainbow is almost impossible, however. The Kamloops rainbow subspecies spawns in the spring, the domestic Wisconsin strain spawns in the fall, the domestic Shasta strain spawns in the winter, and, while 7 years is usually given as a maximum life span, some of the unsullied Alaskan strains live to 12 years or more. There has also been a continuous recruitment of different domestic stocks in many river systems over a long period, plus natural hybridization with the golden and cutthroat trout in water throughout the western United States.

Native only to western North America, *Salmo gairdneri* was long ago given a passport to all the clear-flowing waters of the world, places as far removed as the Urubamba, the sacred river of the Incas that rises at an altitude among the clouds and then plunges past the ruins of Machu Picchu before raging down the eastern slopes of the Andes into the Amazon. If you have lungs like bellows and can run behind a hooked trout along almost perpendicular rapids, fishing that river is a fascinating experience. The Urubamba makes Oregon's turbulent McKenzie River look like a leaky faucet. There are also unnamed lakes in the ridges that still hold 20-pound trout.

While the presence of rainbows in New Zealand is by now legendary, their southernmost latitude is in the Kerguelen Islands opposite Antarctica (which is hard to find unless you turn the globe upside down). One of the most successful introductions in recent history occurred at Lake Nahuel Huapi in Argentina. Originally planted with rainbow trout in 1901, the lake produced fabulous brown trout but only ho-hum rainbow fishing; in fact, the rainbows led a monklike existence at benthic depths and were caught only in modest sizes by deep trolling. Then, in 1965, Argentina imported rainbow eggs from Denmark, which is about as logical as Tokyo importing cars from Detroit. Of course, Denmark originally secured its rainbows from the United States and made trout farming into one of its leading export food industries. This highly pampered stock, which I sampled in the meadow streams of Jutland one summer with artist Svend Saabye, was reminiscent of the precision-tooled drones New York's Cortland hatchery turned out in the 1930s—seemingly bred for quick delivery to the skillet, they displayed all the fighting instincts of Roberto Duran in his infamous eighth round with Sugar Ray Leonard. But the rainbows that were hatched at the federal fish station in Bariloche apparently had Peter Benchley's great white shark in their bloodline. According to Dr. Miguel de Lourdes Baiz, one macho male brood fish bit a tourist on the forefinger as he innocently pointed at the trout in a holding pool.

The day I visited de Lourdes Baiz, he was busy installing screens over the pools because some of the trout kept jumping onto the bank in blind panic every time anybody walked by. This was the same problem that Seth Green mentioned of his Caledonia hatchery in 1874—generations of domestication had yet to breed out that wild reaction to escape. After the fish from Hamlet's mad kingdom were stocked, the change that occurred in Lake Nahuel

Huapi's fishing by 1972 was so radical that local anglers actually believed a new species of trout had evolved. These silvery, deep-bodied, emerald-backed fish went on a constant rampage chasing baitfish in shallow water. Rainbows up to 26 pounds were taken by fly fishermen casting from shore. They reminded me of the wild Kamloops trout of British Columbia, but their spiritual resemblance to a bright steelhead won the name game, so its Spanish synonym *plateado* now separates those rainbows found in the littoral zone from the benthic population. It's possible that the plateado originated in one of Denmark's saltwater hatcheries, and untangling its genesis is a near impossibility.

But there is another element in trout fishing that cannot be measured with tape or scale. I remember our numerous trips to the very top of the Gros Ventre River in Wyoming. There was, and perhaps still is, a population of small rainbows in that river, each with lavender parr marks in perfect heart shapes. Patti called them her Valentine trout. I don't believe we ever caught a fish bigger than 10 inches, but the sheer beauty of the place—with wildflowers surrounding meadow pools, and moose and elk roaming nearby—is beyond my capacity for wielding language. And the first thing that comes to mind about Chile, a country that is laced with rainbow trout streams, is not the fishing, which I knew at its best, but the crisp roasted lamb the *boateros* cooked over an open fire, the good red wines, and the great ripe peaches. Two years ago Keith Gardner and I fished the Morice River in British Columbia, and while I recall catching some nice steelhead, it was the sapphire-blue pools, tall timber, and granite ledges cloaked in morning fog above milepost 32 that made the trip special. It's a wild stream that leaps and roars in its den and, sadly, will soon be tamed by civilization.

Then there is the learning experience through other,

perhaps wiser eyes. I once made a movie on steelhead fishing for the National Film Board of Canada. During the three-week-long shooting, I enjoyed the company of a Kwakiutl Indian guide named Phil. At our lunch break one day we were sitting on a high bank when a group of steelhead, maybe a dozen in all, tried to ford the shallow bar at the stream mouth during a rapidly falling tide. The fish milled around with their backs out of water, dashed halfway across the bar, found virtually no water, and then turned back again. It was strange behavior for any predator-conscious migrant in bright daylight. Finally the fish plunged ahead and, wiggling violently on wet bellies, churned those last few yards into the deeper riffle above. I asked Phil why the steelhead didn't wait for a rising tide. His answer, though allegorical, could not be faulted. He looked at me as though I were asking Albert Einstein to correct a high school algebra paper.

"The swimmers, led by their chief, come from remote villages under the sea. They send their scouts ahead, and if the scouts do not safely pass, the other swimmers will not come. It has always been so."

I didn't ask Phil how the scouts sent the good word back to the villages. It somehow reminded me of that classic explanation that Louis Armstrong used when asked about the meaning of jazz: "If you got to ask, baby, you ain't never gonna know."

Clinic

There is a vast difference in angling techniques for rainbow trout at various geographical locations—from dainty match-the-hatch dry-fly work on the Big Delaware or the Henrys Fork to casting salmon-egg imitations and even hair mice on Alaskan rivers. The steelhead form of rainbow is perhaps more orthodox in preferring bushy dry flies in #10 to #6 sizes, with wet flies from #8 to #2 in summer, and from #4 to #3/0 in winter streams. An all-around steelhead outfit would be an 8½- or 9-foot rod calibered for lines in 8-weight double, triangle, or forward tapers floating, an 8-weight sinking tip, and 9-weight intermediate-sinking, and fast-sinking shooting heads. The necessity for different lines is to get the fly to its most productive depth, from surface to bottom, which in big coastal rivers is a great variable according to season. Obviously, you won't need all these lines on any one occasion, but stored on extra spools they require very little space in your fishing kit. The ability to swim a fly at the right depth is the key to successful steelhead fishing.

Rainbow trout tackle

4

WHEN TWO ARE BETTER THAN ONE

In 1852, it was not considered unusual to use a "strap" of 20 wet flies on one leader. Gentlemen anglers of that period had no intention of catching 20 fish at a clip, but, with a handsome assortment of duns and hackles floating on the current, it seemed logical that one or two trout would find something of interest. Not too many years ago one of the largest trout ever taken from our much-fished Beaverkill River in New York fell to a nymph that was one of twelve flies an ambitious angler was casting—all at once. As an admirer of the crafty brown trout I found this hard to believe, but the facts were clearly established. So perhaps our forefathers knew something about fly fishing that his-

torians failed to record. When the 20-fly cast was in its
heyday, a chap named W. C. Stewart was passing the word
that if you cast upstream instead of down you'd clobber
more fish. It doesn't take much imagination to visualize the
poor angler attempting cast after cast in an upstream direction—with 19 dropper flies beating the air—and then drifting back to his boots almost immediately. Downstream, the
20 flies would take care of themselves. But Stewart made
a strong pitch for casting against the current (his book, *The
Practical Angler,* went through seventy editions) and subsequently conned his disciples into clipping off dropper after
dropper.

There was a generation of anglers on the Catskill
streams at the turn of the century that fished three and four
wet flies at a time—all the time. They would make their
casts across- and downstream, then skip the flies back over
the surface; this was a simple, practical way of telling the
trout that here was something to eat. The effectiveness of
such a direct approach was lost as each crop of new anglers
appeared—the brown trout replaced the brook trout, and
the fly-fishing lore of chalkstreams clouded American waters. People were now educated to using a single floating
fly, and in this pursuit of classic form they forgot the simple
tricks that filled baskets a decade before.

In modern trouting, I'm inclined to believe that one
catches as many or more fish by using only one fly and
concentrating on working it just right. This is especially
true of dry-fly fishing. But all fly fishing is not devoted to the
trout, the dry fly, and ideal conditions. A great deal of time
is spent casting one fly in water where two would be more
appropriate. Occasionally you'll find somebody fishing two
floaters or a pair of wet flies on one cast, and less frequently
you'll meet a three- and four-wet-fly angler. The apparent
reason for fishing more than one fly is to give the trout a
choice—just as the strap artists did in Stewart's day.

There is sufficient evidence in angling literature to indicate that using more than one fly is a sound thesis; we read of anglers who used a Brown Hackle and a Gray Hackle on a single cast, and the trout hit the Gray Hackle every time, whether it was used as a tail fly or a dropper. In more than one instance the angler has used a quartet of flies, and no matter where the killing pattern was located, his trout would find it. I have never experienced this kind of selectivity, but I have managed to creel a few good fish by using three wet flies when a single fly went untouched.

When fished together, a number of flies can be as deadly an attractor to trout as a herring "grapevine" is to tuna fish. H. A. Rolt tells us that professional fishermen on the Tweed and Clyde use 9 flies on their leaders, and that French anglers use from 8 to 10 gaudy patterns for fishing on the River Ain. Personally I have no desire to throw such a string of flies in my trout waters, but the use of two- and three-fly casts is an important part of practical angling. You can catch fish that wouldn't otherwise be caught.

For example, years ago it produced my first 30-inch rainbow on a dry fly. This happened on the Brooks River in Alaska, where trout of that size are not nearly as common as we'd like to believe, and where rainbows are accustomed to eating more sizable items of food than a floating insect. Yet the great fish came to one of a pair of bivisibles skipped in flat water. After trying him with orthodox wet- and dry-fly casts upstream and down, I remembered a stunt Dan Todd taught me years before. On summer evenings when the running sedge and elophilia moths covered the Delaware, Dan would fish two bushy flies downstream and then skip them back over the water. His only reason for fishing this way was to stir the fish up—draw their attention to something easily caught. The sedge and the moth flicked about so fast that they seldom brought rises from the larger fish. My Alaskan rainbow was probably busy getting his belly full of salmon eggs, because he lay at the edge of a swarm of sockeyes, ignoring cast after cast. I made up one of Dan's two-fly rigs and on the fourth or fifth throw the trout left bottom with a mean look in his eye. He sculled behind the dancing bivisibles and then bolted at the nearest one. Which one I can't remember.

The double-bivisible cast is a good one in any kind of water for any insect-feeding fish. If you want some really fast action try them on a long leader when you're fishing with a downstream wind. The flies literally get off the surface and flit around when you raise your rod and strip in line. On big rivers in mountain country where there's a firm draft of air, I've had a pair of flies in constant motion all day long. To get at trout in really rough water, where an ordinary upstream cast would be sucked under, simply flick the flies in those glassy pockets and let them bounce where the fish is certain to be. This brings some smashing aerial strikes at times, and is by all odds one of the most valuable two-fly tricks.

Under different circumstances, two wet flies can be exceptionally good. On our Catskill streams we cast this rig across current, and, holding the rod high, strip the line back with definite short strokes. The slim form of a sunken pattern skims through the surface rather than skipping over it, both flies making a faint V-shaped wake, similar to the trail left by beetles and water boatmen. By holding the rod up most of the line will be off the water and a very lifelike retrieve is possible. This is most effective in evening stream fishing and was the cast that made old Pop Robbins famous on the Beaverkill. Pop was accused of many kinds of witchcraft in his day, but actually his phenomenal successes were based on this direct approach. Over on the Neversink, where currents are stronger and the water bigger, John Pope made his reputation by skimming three big wet flies into the choppers of a waiting trout. With the resignation that is the final courage of old age, Uncle John used a single dry fly just before he died. He reported that the method had "interesting possibilities."

There is a variation of the two wet-fly technique that I call diving-and-bobbing. The chief virtue of this method is that it brings up trout in perfectly dead water. No doubt somebody was fishing this way long before I, but I discovered this two-fly trick quite accidentally.

As we all learn, lake fly fishing is difficult. I think the chief reason for this is that artificial flies have very little inherent action and there's practically nothing the angler can do to simulate life without the help of a current. We can jerk streamers and wet flies through the water and make a fair score, and twitch a dry fly over rising fish, but most people will agree that the quality of the catch depends on how actively the fish are feeding. If the water is glassy, the sun bright, and our fish well fed, each offering is going to be inspected closely, because the trout doesn't have to act quickly. There's no current to take his food away.

I was fishing a small Adirondack pond one afternoon, letting my canoe drift with the breeze. There were a few trout rising from time to time, and I managed to catch one of them on a wet fly. Thinking that the pattern was wrong I tied on a dropper strand and a small, sparsely dressed Gray Hackle. Because it was fresh, and because the hackle was stiff, the new fly wouldn't sink—I gave the line a few pulls to get the fly under, but each time it bobbed up again. After the fourth or fifth pull a fat native smacked it. Obviously the action of the fly was important to the trout, so I cut off the tail fly and put on a similar Gray Hackle. From that moment on business was brisk.

In the diving-and-bobbing method, it is important to use sparsely tied wet hackle patterns. I like a pair of #12 Gray Hackles with yellow bodies. After dousing them in dry-fly oil, shoot the cast out a good distance and let them float quietly for several minutes. When trout are not actively feeding, the quiet float rarely draws a strike, but I suspect that any nearby fish might be looking at the flies. Now take the cast back in foot-long pulls—the flies alternately dive and bob, an action that no amount of rod work can duplicate. Obviously you can do the same thing with a single fly and catch fish. But the two-fly cast has always been more productive for me, and I think this is because the trout are given twice the incentive to commence eating.

Foremost among the attractor rigs is a bucktail and wet-fly combination. The bucktail is tied in as a tail fly, and a small wet pattern is tied up the leader as a dropper fly. It is generally understood that this represents a minnow chasing an insect when the cast is drawn through the water. Interestingly enough, the fish don't always follow the logical sequence of grabbing the bucktail and then the wet fly. Often as not they dash ahead of the "minnow" and take the insect. This two-fly cast supplies the need for a showy fly to get the fish's attention, however, and offers a smaller fly to arouse the appetite. Frankly, I haven't found it very productive on trout, but for bluegill and bass this bucktail attractor is often useful. There is a similar rig made up of a marabou streamer and wet fly that has proven better on our local waters, and if there's any credence to the minnow-chasing-an-insect idea, then this one boasts an insect chasing a minnow, because the wet fly is tied behind the streamer.

Marabou streamers are real fish attractors if properly tied. Unfortunately they are absolutely worthless if the knotmaker uses the wrong part of the plume or too much of it when making the wing. Many marabous simply mat together in the water—these serve no purpose at all. A good one—one that pulses and flutters at the slightest pressure—will excite any kind of gamefish, so much so that this streamer has long been used as a locator fly. Even if your quarry doesn't actually strike he will usually show up behind the marabou, just to look it over; later you can try that spot again, using a more conservative tidbit, like a tiny wet fly, in the place you know your fish to be. This is an ancient method on heavily worked rivers where the angler may have to cover a mile of water for every fish caught.

I don't claim to be the originator of the tandem marabou and wet-fly rig, but it occurred to me a number of years ago that with a small wet fly tied in from the bend of the marabou hook some of the located fish might very well take the fly—if not the attractor. I was fishing the water below Hunter on the Schoharie River that day, and after raising a number of trout who only wanted to play with the marabou, I clinched on a 6-inch strand of nylon and a small hackle pattern. It was an offensive-looking thing, but before long a trout slipped up behind the white ostrich plumes, and, after a few tentative nips at the marabou, he snapped around and swallowed the little wet fly. This is a typical strike and is apparently earned through the provocative action of the streamer.

One of the oldest two-fly casts is a dry-fly and nymph combination. A bushy, high-riding dry fly is tied to the dropper strand, and a small nymph serves at the tail, 4 or 5 feet further down. The dry fly in this case acts as a bobber to indicate the strike. It's often difficult for the novice to detect the touch of a fish when casting sunken flies upstream. Unless the angler has good eyesight and considerable experience the vagrant drift of line and leader is not easily distinguished from a trout's pull. If you use a two-fly cast, however, the dry fly will jerk over or under the surface when the fish stabs the submerged lure. At times a strike will simply halt the floating dry fly, but in moving water the sudden stop is unnatural and obvious even to the beginner.

I seldom use the bobber cast anymore. However, when fishing broken water in poor light, the advanced angler can use this fly to good advantage. A pattern such as the Royal Wulff can be seen quite easily, and, provided the dropper strand is not too long, this fly will respond to the slightest tap down below. With a #14 March Brown Nymph doing the legwork, you have a combination that's hard to beat.

Just recently I had a brief session with some nymphing browns on Upper Mountain Pool in the Beaverkill as the evening turned to dark. It was too late to dry my soggy line, and for all I could see a trout might have nipped at every cast. After I tied on a bobber fly, three trout made their fatal error—signaled by the sensitive dry fly.

The worst light for fly fishing often occurs at midday, and sometimes you get into a position where you must fish blind or not at all. I came down the wrong side of the meadows on the Ausable one day, at a place where I couldn't ford the river. The afternoon sun glared at me like a giant floodlamp, and, since this was a bank fisherman's run, there wasn't much to see beyond the front taper of my line. Three trout had been nymphing along the far side, but my best casts sent them running away. As I walked through the brush I saw a brownie floating just under the surface, feeding freely and dropping foot by foot down the river. In deep, slow streams, trout occasionally work this way when they find a cluster of developing duns. Although the fish wasn't large, the situation was unique. In a matter of seconds the trout had retreated from the one transparent patch of water back into glaring sunlight. I hastily clinched a dropper strand and a Black Gnat dry fly to the middle of the leader, making my cast to the place where I last saw him. The leader straightened out nicely and I could see the fly even as it drifted into the sun. A few shakes of the rod tip brought out more slack as the line swung around to drag, and the bobber fly floated naturally again. By edging another 5 yards along the bank I literally walked with the fly to get a longer drift. Just as the line was about to drag again, my dry fly made a feeble hop. The trout had nudged the nymph and the hook barely set in his lip. A pound of brown trout is not a fish you're likely to remember, but this one came as a soothing lotion to sun-burned eyes.

One of the most important skills in using two flies or more is to make a proper leader. The leader can't be too light and the dropper strands must be properly tied to keep them from tangling. There are a number of knots you can use, but they all slip down the leader sooner or later. However, I would suggest making dropper strands when you build your leaders. I use an extra-long length of the heavier strand when two strands are joined in making the taper. Whether you use the blood knot or the barrel knot, when the knot is finally formed and the stem end is pulled through, it's an easy matter to pull out another 8 or 10 inches. The extra length cannot be pulled from the already formed knot, but should be allowed for when you begin making the tie. If, for instance, my taper calls for a 20-inch strand of .012 and then a 20-inch strand of .010, I use about 28 inches of the .012, which gives me an 8-inch dropper strand. The dropper should always be of the heavier diameter between any two sizes in order that it will stand away from the leader. For the same reason you can-not use too large a fly on the dropper or the weight of the fly will cause a tangle.

None of these casts that I've described is new to angling. Even though our equipment is different from the gear used a century ago we are still searching for the same fish, and they have changed very little. Recently I saw a tapered horsehair line and a set of wet flies that were more than 100 years old. They were perfectly preserved and obviously made by a loving craftsman. If this fellow were to wade my stream tomorrow I suspect we'd be hard put to learn where I began and he left off.

Clinic

While these observations on multiple-fly rigs are three decades old, the practitioners of the art are still plying their craft. A few years ago, I met an angler astream near Gatlinburg, Tennessee, who was fishing a strap of nymphs with great success while my single sunk patterns went begging for strikes. In a more remote enclave, together with Gilbert Drake, I was on the Buna River in Yugoslavia getting nothing but exercise when an angler wading behind us hooked several fine trout, including one that he could barely fit in his landing net. Our curiosity was overwhelming; like the old boy in Tennessee, he was using a half-dozen cream-colored nymphs with a tiny weight crimped to his leader. Personally, I have never graduated beyond the three-fly rig with wet patterns. But fishing a pair of dry flies downstream is worth trying in fast water where the flow is just too strong for upstream wading. In addition to bivisibles, buoyant hair-bodied and winged patterns such as the Irresistible, Rat-Faced McDougall, Sofa Pillow, or Elk-Wing Caddis are perfect for this kind of fishing. The trick is to get a short drift with the flies, then to hold the rod high to create a hopping, skimming action, working the retrieve slowly to tease the trout up. This is especially effective in a downstream wind when you can get the flies jumping in the air. The tail fly should be a size or two larger than the dropper fly for easy casting.

5

THE COUNTRY OF OUR YOUTH

In 1734, the Common Council of what was to be the city of New York passed a law that restricted trout fishing in then popular Collect Pond to "Angling with Angle Rod, Hook and Line, only." Although the island of Manhattan was fissured with ponds and streams, the early settlers had already netted some of these waters to near depletion. During the next two centuries, the ponds were filled, the streams funneled into conduits, and the whole island gradually covered with asphalt. Seemingly, all the ghosts of the past were forever sealed from view. Then, in 1956, when a water main broke on 58th Street and Madison Avenue, plumbing expert Jack Gasnick found a brook trout flopping in the gutter as water poured down the street. Like most of his compatriots who work the city's underground, Mr. Gasnick has taken a variety of fish over the years, including pickerel (which are especially prone to getting lodged in fire hydrants), carp, goldfish, smelt, catfish, and eels. But this was his first trout—possibly a relic from the Turtle Bay Stream, which still meanders under the East 50s. According to Mr. Gasnick, who has since netted trout in the flooded basements of 301 and 325 East 52nd Street, the stream is audible, as it whimpers behind walls and below cellars. Plumbing suppliers and troubleshooters Charles J. Hassel and J. Henry Kling have also collected numerous specimens, adding yellow perch and striped bass to the Big Apple's abysmal checklist. In the eyes of its nomenclator, *Salvelinus fontinalis* is a "fish of the fountains" and indeed, there is modern proof. One brook trout erupted from the outlet pipe of a lobby fountain in a newly built Greenwich Village apartment house, which straddles the site of what once was another productive stream— Minetta Brook. I won't speculate on the underground life of salmonids, as I can't even imagine what the pH of a Manhattan water main might be, and God knows how trout feed or reproduce in a no-photoperiod environment. Maybe they just wander down from the Catskills along some labyrinthian path and get mugged by a bib faucet. The point is, this beautiful native American char should have vanished over most of its original range years ago— but its spirit is indomitable.

The brook trout was the first species to invade the streams being formed by melting ice in the last Pleistocene epoch of the Appalachians. In her master plan, Nature sent along a companion foodfish, the sculpin, who is also tolerant of extremely cold water. As the ice melted, lakes formed below any barrier on the slopes of mountains, and when the water level dropped and currents warmed, fishes such as the minnows and suckers began their upstream journeys. In many places, rock slides and impassable falls now blocked their entry into brook trout habitats in the headwaters. But man, the original Mixmaster, eventually introduced alien brown and rainbow to the native and a variety of problems began. In the social fabric of our trout family, the brookie now hangs by a bare thread. Except for certain isolated strains, it generally has a shorter life span (5 years) than the rainbow (7 years) or the brown trout (10 years). It is more susceptible to angling, and cannot withstand competition from the other species for resting and feeding sites. When you see a hatchet-faced rainbow nipping the belly of a brook trout in swift, corkscrew attacks, it becomes painfully evident who is boss. The rainbow gets the turbulent, food-rich, oxygenated water, while our delicate native gets an inferiority complex and sulks under a remote rock.

Pioneer fish culturist Seth Green probably had the greatest impact on the streams of Appalachia through his experiments with an early-maturing domesticated strain that promised a quick solution to our already declining brook trout populations in the nineteenth century. The intangible, however, was that his stock had a genetic flaw: it also had a short life span. These fish were widely introduced and soon dominated what was left of our "wild" trout fishing. Even Ray Bergman, the Dr. Spock of a whole generation of trout anglers, in writing of his experiences during those "horse and buggy" days in New York waters, felt need of a footnote to the effect that "at this time restocking streams was very uncertain and legal-size fish were not used for this purpose."

Today, brook trout in Eastern upland streams seldom make it beyond 3 years of age with a climax size of about 10 inches. The largest native I ever caught in the Catskills was exactly 14 inches long, and that was back in the 1930s.

I have taken stocked fish of greater size but their only bona fides were a club membership and access to a ton of Trout Chow. During the halcyon era of squaretail fishing in Maine, from the 1880s to the 1920s, 5- to 7-year-old brook trout (weighing 3½ to 5 pounds) were not uncommon. Presumably, some of this genetic stock has survived, as the state continues to produce an occasional trophy fish. In Canada, there are even longer-lived brook trout populations such as the Assinica strain, which attains an age of 10 or more years, and weights of 9 to 11 pounds. However, our native trout lives in a delicate balance everywhere because of habitat destruction and overfishing. There are foam-flecked rivers, running through forests where the logger's axe has never echoed, that hold trophy-size fish, yet any of these could be wiped out tomorrow. Fortunately, enlightened resort operators like Jack Cooper, who honchos the Minipi River camp in Labrador, offer their angling on a catch-and-release basis, which is the only hope for the last frontier.

Ted Williams and I have a long-standing donnybrook over which is the superior gamefish. In his salad days at Fenway Park, Ted batted .400, and as an angler he scores .500 in my book, so when he narrows it down to Atlantic salmon, bonefish, and tarpon, the argument is formidable. I can't tell him how to hit a knuckleball, or cast a fly, nor am I able to squeeze the steelhead in third place. I'm tempted to put the South American dorado in first place, and the sea-run brown trout in second place. Tarpon, no. That's where the magic of a name, like the cut of the emperor's clothes, protects a reputation so well established as to seem inviolate. About the time I put my elbow in the spaghetti sauce, I resort to the old homily that there's more to fishing than the fish. To Ted, this is like sending in a Little League pitcher, right-handed at that. The truth is, I've never been able to make up my mind. If

I named three today, they'd probably be different tomorrow. By his measure, I'd have trouble placing the brook trout in the first ten.

The squaretail may jump gracefully through the air on magazine covers but in reality it usually flops, squirms, and tail-threshes at the surface, seldom becoming airborne. A big brook trout is much more likely to dive for the nearest obstruction in powerful surges, and in the thunderous rapids of a river like Gods, or the Broadback, you have your hands full. And the squaretail learns his lessons badly. He is sometimes seen with a mouthful of rusting flies and broken leaders. I once caught a 5-pounder in a small Quebec lake that had a half-dozen hooks in its jaws; if nothing else, the larger fish have needle-sharp teeth. But this lack of guile may be a point in its favor. There is solace in finding at least one salmonid who occasionally lets me feel that I've learned something about fishing. It's not all that easy in civilized waters, as those natives who survive can be as spooky as any other trout.

For that matter we had a near wipeout one snowy day in a remote Argentinian lake, where huge brookies swam about in plain sight, ignoring every pattern that three anglers could muster. We managed to hook a few but these were charitable fish. The following day, the weather turned bright and warm as we drove south to camp at Lago General Paz. There we caught brook trout in numbers and sizes that still boggle my mind. Fish of over 4 pounds were par for the course, and several exceeded 8 pounds. Johnny Dieckman, who was then International Casting Champion, took one of 9¼ pounds. I doubt if his casting impressed the trout so much as his unflagging devotion to hooking and releasing fish from dawn until dusk. He didn't even stop to eat. Originally from Maine, these trout were planted in a noncompetitive vacuum during the 1920s where an abundance of crayfish, freshwater crabs, and galaxiias minnows composed a rich food supply. I don't know what the present status of Lago General Paz might be; on my last visit we had an access problem with Chilean border guards at the productive outlet end of the lake. Our guide was a suspected gun runner (which he later bragged about) and the *soldados* were as friendly as snarling cougars. We decamped with self-congratulations. So whether a record trout is possible at Paz, as has been rumored, must, for me at least, wait in the hold file.

In the year 1916, Dr. William J. Cook caught a 14½ pound brook trout on the Nipigon River in Ontario. This region was famous long before the skilled doctor began his piscatorial operations. His world record is well documented. The other celebrated brook trout, said to be equally as large, was captured by Senator Daniel Webster in 1823. Webster's fish, immortalized in a Currier & Ives lithograph, and with its dimensions traced, then carved into a weathervane for the Brookhaven Presbyterian church, makes a charming legend (it was said that the senator got up during a sermon and hastened to the stream, where he hooked the great trout while a gathering congregation cheered or chorused hallelujahs) but the facts are somewhat confused. Invocation from the Scriptures may have been part of Webster's technique, but where did he catch the fish? In one version, it was the Nissequogue River and by another, more logical account, Carman's River— one on the north and the other on the south shore of Long Island, New York. The size of the weathervane was also deliberately exaggerated by its artisan for better visibility. And while both streams have access to salt water, an environment where brown and rainbow grow to record sizes, an anadromous brook trout seldom attains a weight of over 5 pounds even after debauching in the bounty of the sea. Worse yet, he comes back looking like a used car salesman in a mail-order suit. Although Webster's fish was entered

into our *Congressional Record* many years later, it appears to be an exorcised hobgoblin, lending verisimilitude to an amusing incident—exactly what we'll never know. In 1961, the church was moved to nearby Bellport, where both the original weathervane and the Currier & Ives version of the faithful black slave Apaius Enos netting Webster's fish (as he captionally exclaims "We hab you now, sar!") can be seen at the Bellport Historical Society Museum.

The indomitable spirit of a brook trout is challenged in a river like Gods. From its top at Kanuchuam Rapids down through Big Bear to Red Sucker, the deep pools and glides give way to bouldery, torrential chutes, which only the expert Cree canoemen can negotiate in their 20-foot canoes. The river narrows and virtually explodes in pebbles and foam at Farting Rapids (the Cree language is often pictographic) and it's a miracle that any fish survive. Below Red Sucker, the river becomes broader and shallower, and here "small" trout of 2 to 3 pounds are more numerous. From where Gods joins the Hayes River down to York Factory the water is silted and the mosquito-drenched country dismally barren on the shores of Hudson Bay. Although the upper 50 miles of Gods is larded with stoneflies, there are few places where one can successfully fish with floating patterns; in most trophy waters you must send down a big streamer for consistent results. If there is any chance for a rise, it usually occurs in the evening; this, in my experience, is generally true of northern trout country. Morning fishing is best resolved by an extra hour in the sack and another bout with the flapjacks and bacon. At dusk, you might find surface-feeding squaretails in eddies and backwaters; then, a bushy Brown Wulff—aimed at a cruiser—works its old magic.

In the northern refugium of *fontinalis* it appears to me that the largest fish are still found in headwater populations. This is not only true in Gods (where we searched out spawning areas for a study being made by Dr. Bert Kooyman, Manitoba's director of fisheries, in 1960) but in other streams we subsequently visited by helicopter along the Hudson Bay shore. Many of the smaller river mouths are badly shoaled or blocked by gravel accumulated over the centuries, and only floods or extreme tides make the passage of fish possible. In this land, where all streams flow north, one might assume that the more "remote" pools downstream hold larger trout, but the reverse is more likely. You can catch tremendous numbers of 2- to 3-pound sea-run brookies in some estuaries, but after a while one is apt to feel like a racehorse plodding a milk route. For trophy fishing you must still go inland to the "fountains." This brings me to another kind of brook trout fishing, which in some respects is the best of all.

Ben Hecht once said that the finest country in the world is Youth, and I suppose if that's gone, its corollary is the country of our youth. When my daughter was about six years old, we began visiting a certain brook together, far away from the road, that flows down a mountain through dark hemlocks and windfall tangles before joining the river. A stranger wouldn't know the brook exists because, in the last 100 yards or so, its voice has been silenced where it flows under a vast pile of gravel deposited by countless floods. But up the mountain, for about five miles, there is a series of fern-fringed pools connected by bubbly runs and even infant waterfalls. We would pack our sandwiches and spend the day probing greeny pockets with dry flies to find colorful little jewels that sparkled and danced in the sunshine. I had made Susan a rod from a 4-foot fiberglass tip section and, although her casts were limited, there were always a few innocents willing to splash at her Coachman. The fishing didn't matter, really. Often we'd just sit on a ledge and watch the trout, who in the pale amber of the pool looked like Chinese mandarins in their jade robes, speckled with red gems, as they swayed in some stylized ritual. The food talk of thrushes and grosbeaks came as grace notes to the melody of the stream. There were salamanders and giant toadstools to admire, grouse to flush, watercress and blackberries to eat, chipmunks to feed bread to, and a hundred other reasons to make that uphill journey. Once, in a drought summer, we followed the brook with dip nets, rescuing those fingerling that were left stranded in drying shallow riffles and moving them into permanent pools. I can still see her blond head bobbing under the rhododendron as Susan netted a fish and ran frantically for the nearest deep spot shouting "Daddy, I got one!" I realized then that our brook was literally what philosophers had in mind when they spoke of a stream of consciousness, where a moral obligation is recognized— no matter how abstract. Two decades have passed and nothing much has changed, except now, on the homeward trek, I don't have to carry Susan piggyback anymore, nor empty her pockets of salamanders. Nor dry her pants.

That beautiful lady sits patiently and waits for the old man to get his second wind.

Clinic

Back in 1949, Don Gapen of Nipigon, Ontario, introduced
me to a fly of his own design called the Muddler Minnow.
Today, this pattern and all its variations virtually hold a
cult status, but when I first showed one to Dan Bailey on
the Yellowstone River his reaction—"What the hell is that
thing?"—was typical. Gapen's brainchild, tied to imitate a
sculpin (a natural associate and food of the brook trout in
its native waters), proved to be a phenomenal success not
only for squaretails but for just about every species that
takes a fly—even permit and bonefish have fallen to the
Muddler. The beauty of this pattern is that it can be fished
wet or dry; on the surface it probably suggests a grasshop-

per, dragonfly, or stonefly. My favorite way of fishing the
fly as a dry is by casting across stream and working it in
short twitches—in effect an injured minnow or large insect
struggling against the current. When the line has arced
directly downstream, I retrieve it in more emphatic pulls,
creating a diving-and-bobbing action, stopping the movement between each pull. I also use weighted Muddlers to
scratch bottom on big rivers. I count the Muddler and the
Adams dry fly as essential to every trout anglers' kit.

6

THE BEAUTIFUL DANCER

The early French settlers on the Saint Lawrence River called the smallmouth bass *achigan,* an Algonquin word meaning "ferocious." I don't think that would sell on a summer's day on Forty Acre Shoal when bass are yawning in the face of a Rapala. But even the Latin species name *Micropterus dolomieui* is a Gallic screw-up meaning "Dolomieu's small-fin" because Lacepede, who first described the fish in 1802, had at hand a single deformed specimen with a torn dorsal. Dolomieu was a French naturalist contemporary of Lacepede, so science is not very enlightening. For my money, the only man who ever came close to putting the smallmouth bass in two words was a jolly Russian who invaded the Delaware River back in the 1950s.

Maybe George Washington crossed it, but Aleksandr Fyodorovich Kerensky, the last prime minister of Russia (who hastily departed office during the Bolshevik revolution) fished it—albeit a minor historical note. Alex was an occasional angling pal of mine. He was eighty years old when I first met him in New York and built like a Brahma bull with an earthshaking basso profundo voice that he exercised frequently by singing Russian folk songs while casting his *Plooky mee-no*. There weren't many spinning lures on the market at that time but you may recall the Plucky, a little jointed rubber minnow, which Alex often wore around his ears. He had a tendency to release his casts too early, sending the lure straight overhead. Between his singing and his casting, those Delaware smallmouths played it cool. But one evening the impossible happened. Alex delivered a *Plooky* flat out and caught an almost 5-pound bass, a trophy size even in the then lush pastures around Lordville. Naturally, this was reason for a song which emerged in mounting crescendos, probably shattering eardrums on the Pennsylvania shore. The name of the tune in Russian doesn't exactly sound the way it reads, *"Krasiviy Tantsor,"* but it translates to "The Beautiful Dancer." I can't picture Ray Scott announcing a tournament for beautiful dancers without swallowing a mouthful of fruit-flavored jelly worms. Yet I think Alex, seeing with eyes that familiarity had had no chance to glaze, captured the spirit of the fish pirouetting and leaping in snappy kicks over a riffle sparkling gold in the sunset.

The smallmouth bass has always been high on my list of favorites, but for all the years I have faithfully fished them—and the total score would run well into the thousands—I've taken very few over 5 pounds in weight. In the boom days of Dale Hollow I lucked into a 7½-pound smallmouth and have never shaded it since; plenty of 4s and

4½s and a few 6s but that's where I'm stuck. However, from muzzle to butt plate the smallmouth is game at any size. While snorkeling in the Buffalo River in Arkansas, I watched a little bass trying to eat a big crayfish. This baby smallmouth had his lunch cornered under a rock and each time the bass stuck his snout inside, the old crawdad grabbed him by the nose and held fast. It obviously hurt because his dorsal spines stood erect and his pectorals vibrated like a hummingbird's wings. When I paddled away about ten minutes later, the little guy was still studying that pocket like a pool player circling the table in a bad run.

Popular bass literature is devoted almost entirely to crank baits, spinner baits, plastic worms, chuggers, and other lures suitable for the baitcasting and spinning rods. Fly fishing is a minority pastime, and the dry fly for smallmouth bass is as obscure as a tract on the Ptolemic celestial

hypothesis. Yet I can think of few gamefish that provide more fun when taken on light tackle with floating flies. In the right waters, under suitable conditions, you will enjoy soul-stirring rises and a quality of sport that would give the most passionate trout fisherman pause. When smallmouths are on the take, it's not unusual to release 50 or 60 in a day's angling on rivers like the James or Shenandoah in Virginia, South Branch of the Potomac in West Virginia, the Susquehanna in Pennsylvania, the Snake in Washington, or in lakes such as Spednic in Maine, Rainy in Ontario, or Magaguadavic in New Brunswick.

I began fishing for smallmouths with the dry fly when I was a teenager working on a farm in Margaretville, New York. In those days the East Branch of the Delaware held a substantial population of bass, especially in those mossy-ledge-bordered pools between Arena and Shavertown, an area that has since been innundated by the Pepacton Reservoir. Actually, it was famed as brown trout water and at first my bass were minor "accidents" that came to little dry flies religiously fished upstream on a drag-free natural drift. I didn't suspect that smallmouths were more prone to a different technique and, frankly, didn't care. I lived in a trout-oriented village where the serious pursuit of bass was demeaning Holy Writ. Even getting a tooth pulled during a mayfly hatch was impossible. Our only dentist, Doc Faulkner, would be on the river. Doc once broke his leg and was wading the next day in a plaster cast. Among my peers *Micropterus dolomieui* was just one of nature's extravagances like a praying mantis, or a cow with six tits.

One night, while fishing a big dry fly downstream, a nocturnal practice that was sanctified locally by the legendary John Alden Knight, I hooked what I thought to be the world's biggest brown trout. To me, fishing in the dark always had a disembodied quality (probably the dumbest exercise is bonefishing at night) and all that tuggin' and splashin' made me lose my grip on reality. The fish peeled off 25 yards of enameled fly line and hung tough. I eventually horsed my prize up on the quickstones and it turned out to be a 4-pound smallmouth. From that moment on, *I* was hooked.

Dry-fly fishing for smallmouth bass is one of the easiest disciplines to master. It's seldom technically hobbled by the need for hatch-matching, and it doesn't require expert casting to toss a fly 30 or 40 feet, which is about the normal requirement. Unlike air-resistant bass bugs, the dry fly can be delivered with a very light rod and line. I use an 8-foot, 1½-ounce graphite rod with a #6 double taper and against this featherweight tackle, hooking a 2-pound bass is like connecting with an electric circuit. I love to feel a rod bend in pulsing arcs, and the heavy gear so often used for smallmouths is way out of proportion for a modest-size gamefish generally taken in open water. If there's any trick at all to bringing bass up to a floater it's in using a "meaty" pattern like a fat-bodied Irresistible on a #6 hook. When fishing dries in a river the most effective approach is to cast across the current to get a short dead drift that positions the fly near a likely hold, then twitch it back over the surface as the fly makes its swing. A double taper line with a 9-foot 2X leader creates very little disturbance. By comparison, a weight-forward line will simply nail the fly to the water and you won't achieve that lifelike skipping action. Smallmouths often take on the drift but the great majority strike when the fly is activated, tippy-toeing on well-oiled hackles.

Only rarely have I found bronzebacks to be selective. A mayfly or caddis emergence can trigger wild surface activity, such as the late June and early July hatches of Green Drakes on the lakes of southeastern Maine, but even the bass are opportunistic feeders. Wind-blown terrestrials such as flying ants, crickets, spiders, beetles, grasshoppers, moths, and bees are meat and potatoes to the smallmouth, and cruising fish will gobble whatever fortune serves. When dragonflies and damselflies are numerous, a pattern with a slim silhouette like a greased Muddler (the exception to my fat rule), skimmed on the surface in fast pulls, can be dynamite. These "darning needles" repeatedly flit over the water to drop their eggs. The damselfly sometimes swims underwater to oviposit, which causes the bass to race to the top in slashing rises, often nailing hovering insects on the wing. One day when the air was full of dragonflies, Bob Elliot of the Maine Development Commission and I caught countless smallmouths in Keg Lake, including several 4½-pound fish. We not only had numerous double hookups but twice I had a big bass take the fly before it hit the water. In that diamond clarity we could see the fish scampering around like starving mice in a cheese factory.

Wildlife artist Ned Smith tipped me off on the great dry-fly fishing that occurs on the Susquehanna in mid-September when flying ants inspire bass to feed hungrily on the surface. Autumn is a beautiful time to be on any river and, with cooling and low water levels, it produces some of the best fly fishing of the year. Fortunately, we allowed ourselves a week, because the first day or so was spent banging away at bouldery riffles with little success. My good friend Wally Exman, who always accomplishes the unusual, caught a large white sucker on a dry fly, then was stung by a big madtom while doing the scientific bit of studying the bottom side of a rock for God knows what. It left a permanent lump on his finger.

There is a structure pattern to fishing bass streams, just as there is in lakes; at certain times the fish will concentrate in deep or shallow pools, the tails of pools, in the riffles, over different types of substrates, and in currents of specific velocities. Food availability and water temperature dictate these movements. We finally began taking good fish in two or three feet of water, always opposite a grassy bank, over coarse gravel (about the diameter of a walnut) and in very moderate current. From then on, it was a matter of finding similar locations as we boated downstream. Some hot spots were only a hundred yards long, yet loaded with feeding bass ready to grab a twitched floater. During the dog days of summer the Susquehanna fish—unlike those of some other bass rivers—go down into highly oxygenated pools where the dry fly is impotent, but in the fall season the Susquehanna offers excellent top-water sport.

Obviously, dry-fly fishing for smallmouth bass has its limits. To promise daily success is as foolhardy as to tell a kid he'll become an NFL champion if he eats his daily bowl of Total. The game collapses on most lakes when the fish retreat to deep water. You might on occasion find a school feeding over shallow midlake shoals, or surfacing for a mayfly hatch in the evening, but you'll have to get out the plastic worms, grubtails, spinner baits, and sonics to do business under a summer sun. During these marginal periods, in addition to the fly rod, I take along an ultralight spinning outfit (4 pound test) to comb the ledges and dropoffs, an activity that is no less sporting than dry-fly fishing even though the bonus of visible strikes is missing. On many rivers you can achieve fishable depths of 4 to 8 feet with a sinking line using weighted nymphs and streamer flies, but this becomes a laborious process when you are casting blind in a lake where the bass are down 15 feet or more. To me, ultralight is an ideal alternate method in terms of water coverage and a lot more fun than handicapping the speedy play of the fish with long lengths of essentially heavy fly line.

Each year I sally forth to Maine with Keith Gardner for the sole purpose of consuming the state's lobster supply and satisfying our appetites for fast fly-rod action, which in

either event is like trying to remove freckles with a gum
eraser. (Keith, who is the astute editor of *Fishing World*,
recently surpassed Wally Exman's dry-fly sucker by catching a large freshwater mussel on a wet fly. The bivalve was
not snagged but hooked fairly in the mouth at the opposite
end of its siphon.) We usually visit a half dozen different
lakes; one (which shall remain nameless as there's a road
into it now, already studded with beer cans) can be reached
from another lake by a slow 8- or 9-mile boat ride down a
narrow wilderness stream. We could be at our destination
in one-tenth of the time by driving but then it wouldn't be
the same. The stream meanders between low spruce-clad
hills, through cattails and wild rice where the bird life is like
some exotic aviary. Maine's bald eagles have come back in
recent years and it's a joy to see them riding the thermals.
There are birch-chomping beavers and often moose doing
their aquatic thing and without this prelude the whole point
of the trip is lost. The fish we come to admire and release are
seldom big but they are uncannily beautiful bass.

I have read many biological descriptions of the smallmouth species, and had to write a few myself for ency-
clopedias and field guides. It's easy enough to recite the
scale counts and spiny and soft fin-ray counts. We can say
the bass has three horizontal stripes on a conical head and
nine or more dark bars on a moderately compressed ovate
body with small ctenoid scales extending on the cheek. It
also has bands of villiform teeth on the jaws, prevomer,
and palatines. These features are dear to the heart of a
taxonomist who can reduce them to a meristic formula. But
somehow I don't *see* the fish. It's like describing man as a
featherless biped. We take bass in "our" lake that beggar
description—rusty bronze and striped like a zebra with
pale blue cheeks and a dusky butter-yellow belly sporting
orange pectorals—as pretty as any brook trout in their
mannequin perfection.

Though the fish over in Third and Fourth Machias Lakes become sooty-colored with age, still the spirit is there. It's always there, from banner-tailed fingerling to potbellied 12-year-old who can read the label on a Mepps.

Aleksandr Fyodorovich Kerensky had the gift of tongues. Historians say he was "one of few orators capable of directing the passions of crowds." With that awesome voice I can believe it. So I humbly submit, his two-word description not only surpasses Lacepede, who got it wrong anyhow, but it might cast a long shadow over the green paths of the future. I hope in this age when a "hawg" swims with a price on his head, the beautiful dancer will not escape your notice.

Clinic

One can make some general observations about river smallmouths: they are seldom found in fast currents, although they may hold on the lee side of boulders, or objects such as downed timber, undercuts, ledges, or stumps near the *edge* of a strong flow. Bear in mind, however, that a location with a strong current in the month of May can dwindle to a modest flow by September and provide excellent fishing where it did not exist in the early season. Smallmouths avoid sand, silt, and mud bottoms and prefer gravel or rock substrates with a moderate current. During the hottest part of summer they may enter cold tributaries when the main river exceeds optimum temperatures, or concentrate at the mouths of feeder streams. In the course of a day's fishing, a pattern should become apparent as to the type of water that is most productive. Some of the clues may be ashore, such as the grassy banks in relation to coarse gravel (as described on the Susquehanna), which could reflect food availability, or even spring seepage. At times overhanging trees provide an abundance of insect life such as caterpillars, ants, and beetles that periodically swarm along the river.

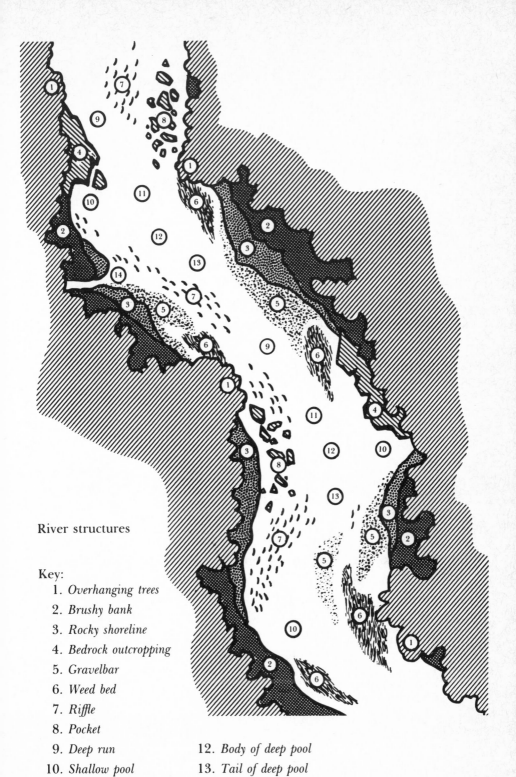

River structures

Key:

1. *Overhanging trees*
2. *Brushy bank*
3. *Rocky shoreline*
4. *Bedrock outcropping*
5. *Gravelbar*
6. *Weed bed*
7. *Riffle*
8. *Pocket*
9. *Deep run*
10. *Shallow pool*
11. *Head of deep pool*
12. *Body of deep pool*
13. *Tail of deep pool*
14. *Mouth of incoming stream*

7

THAT FATAL FASCINATION

One of the greatest thrills a fly fisherman can experience is to take a really large trout on the dry fly. But the odds are heavy agaïnst the angler because very few fish of 5 pounds or more are ever going to swim after bugs in broad daylight, and if they should it would only be under unusual circumstances. I think the best proof was in the results of *Field & Stream*'s former fishing contest, where year after year most of the fly-casting-division winners were caught on streamers or bucktails. The most popular patterns, incidentally, were the Coachman Bucktail, Green Marabou, White Marabou, Mickey Finn, and that old favorite, the black-and-white bucktail. The winners included Eastern and Western rainbow trout, browns, and brook trout. So it's safe to say that the nation's fattest trout turn to something substantial when they get serious about eating, and that means minnows or fingerling gamefish.

Early in my fishing career I fished with bucktails and streamer flies almost exclusively. They are easy to tie and, in the eyes of a youngster, easy to associate with catching fish. In that water on the East Branch of the Delaware from Shinhopple down the main branch to Port Jervis were some of the greatest bass pools in the country. It didn't take long to find that simple brown-and-white and black-and-white bucktails, which represented the many brook minnows and shiners, were more effective than the fancy dressings that Dan Todd copied from the catalogs of New England tackle houses. Our fishing was distinctly and to-tally different. We used the standard thin silver or gold tinsel body with these wings for trout bucktails and the fat full-bodied red, yellow, or black wool bodies ribbed with tinsel for bass.

Delaware smallmouths like a fuller shape and a bit more color in their bucktails. To make closer imitations of certain minnows we used hackle featherwings, and these streamers had a definite role in late-summer, low-water fishing. The barred killifish was represented in patterns tied with a barred-rock hackle feather. The pronounced dark vertical stripes closely simulate the markings of this species. A pattern such as the Grizzly Gray streamer is close to the ones we made.

Then there were the bridled minnows, a group of minnows collectively called "pin minnows" in Vermont and New Hampshire, as we later learned; these have a dark, in many cases pronounced, stripe running down the lateral line. Here the badger hackle featherwing is the minnow's counterpart, particularly that feather known as "golden" badger. Most of the laterally marked minnows are straw-colored overall, with a silvery belly.

The Northern sculpin turned up in bass and trout stomachs so often that Dan and I worked hard on getting a useful imitation, and these patterns revolved around strips of hen pheasant wing laid over bucktail to create that mottled brown form. Eventually we decided that the only important thing about the sculpin was the way he swam in short hops and darts along the bottom. This discovery busted Hale's Eddy wide open one morning when we caught about 20 bass and trout by fishing the fly in that manner.

Some white or yellow is essential in all bucktails that I use. These are the backgrounds for any other color. In fact, an all-white or all-yellow bucktail with tinsel body is often good, and in my experience this is not true of black or red, except when they are tied with marabou wings. But first in importance is black combined with white, then brown-and-white, and then white combined with bright red. In waters where dace are abundant I like brown combined with yellow, using a gold tinsel body. Black-and-yellow or black combined with orange is effective sometimes, but in the streams I fish regularly these two wings are not nearly as good as the others. Blue and green are poor takers unless combined with white in a regular hackle featherwing, and even then I've found such dressings sporadic in their results on our Delaware watershed. Yet the blues and greens are of first importance farther east, especially in Maine. Here patterns such as the Supervisor, Green King, Nine-Three, Green Ghost, and Barnes Special soar and swoop through local legend. But their sphere of influence becomes spotty as the angler heads west.

The featherwing streamer is less popular in the Pacific area, where the minnow fly is used chiefly for steelhead and coho salmon. A hairwing is much more durable between the jaws of either one. Much of this fishing is done in salt and brackish water where large forage fish are common and the hairwing is more easily tied and more readily cast in 4- and 5-inch lengths. As a result, the tall-tree country leans to patterns such as the Candlefish, Skykomish Sunrise, Coronation, the late Jim Pray's Owl-Eyed Optic and Thor Bucktail, the Umpqua Special, and Fred Reed's Orange Steelheader. There are featherwing streamers peculiar to the West such as the Chappie by C. O. Franklin and the Spruce by Roy Donnelly, but by and large the trend over the years has been to hairwings—bucktail and polarbear hair. Each new watershed develops its own patterns, which is as it should be.

My first fly rod was a very long one, a seamed tubular steel affair not unlike a series of umbrella staves jointed together. I don't remember how long it was, but I did have good control over my line because of the length, a factor that is usually missing in my streamer work today. Now that I own a closetful of rods I never seem to have the right one with me when the time comes to play a minnow fly through difficult places. The ideal rod for fishing streamer flies would be about 9½ feet in length, but such a rod, being adapted to nothing but streamer flies, has a practical disadvantage. As close as I have been able to come to the long rod, still maintaining maximum capacity in its other functions with the dry and wet fly, is an 8-foot, 8-1/2-inch medium-action. This length has good control over the streamer when working across varying currents. By holding the tip high, most of the belly portion of the line can be eliminated from the surface, thereby reducing drag and permitting a hand-to-fly sensitivity that would be lost with a heavy, submerged line. A rod takes a beating when you're casting a fly as heavy as a bucktail and lifting it out of the water, as is frequently necessary. This is one reason why I always suggest the 8½-foot or even 9-foot rod for the novice.

While my tubular steel rod was only a sad imitation of what a good fly rod should be, the way it handled a bucktail was a pure delight.

Under normal stream conditions, the minnow-type fly is cast across and downstream, allowing the lure to drift with the current. An occasional movement of the rod keeps the bucktail alive and, when all the slack is out of the line, the fly is retrieved back upstream in short pulls. The darting motion of the bucktail should be very short and spaced at regular intervals to simulate a small minnow struggling against the current. Before the cast is fully retrieved, it often pays to let the fly drift back downstream as though dead and then repeat the swim. Remember to keep your rod parallel to the surface and retrieve by stripping the line over your rod-hand finger. Many good fish are missed by anglers who retrieve by swinging the rod around to a position where they can't strike when the fish hits.

In my opinion, the successful use of the streamer and bucktail fly has been limited to a few experienced fishermen who change their strategy with their lures. Random casting with these flies is disappointing because the fish that will take them are not nearly so plentiful as those that will take dry and wet flies. You must first learn to recognize favorable situations. One place, for instance, is in the feeding runs above big still holes where large trout may lie undisturbed during the day. About a half-hour before the sun leaves the water, these trout are active. If a bucktail or streamer is allowed to work in the current, darted here and there but seldom withdrawn, it often gets results. In the middle of the day, if the fly is sunk deep and idled around, allowed to eddy and move in the bottom currents, and seldom retrieved, a big trout can be tantalized. Remember, the fish is baffled by a fly that repeatedly dashes off—it makes trout suspicious if you withdraw the fly suddenly and often. About the time a fish makes up his mind to take it, and they don't always hurry in making up their minds, the average angler pulls the fly out of the water. The secret of fishing a streamer fly is in not hurrying the lure. Big fish are often deliberate in their feeding habits.

The technique for bass is not always the same. In general, we look for river bass in the same places we look for big trout. That the two species use the same shelter is not unusual. On the Delaware River, for instance, many of the largest trout are taken after several bass have been removed from the very same hole. But the bass fisherman using bucktails has more water to play with, because bronze-backs wander around much more than trout do, and frequently in broad daylight they will chase minnows up into water so shallow that their dorsals show above the surface.

On most bass rivers, the fish generally hold toward the heads of the eddies where they can watch the moving water for food. The fly should come to the holding water with the current, the line held carefully cross-stream from the trout's position. The best procedure is to cast the streamer slightly up and across stream, causing the submerged fly to swing down in a curve. It's a good idea to jerk the rod tip as the fly follows the natural path of the line, and strip in short lengths, to exaggerate the action. Let the fly drift in this manner until it reaches a point directly downstream, and then work it back, until the line is shortened and you can pick it up for the next cast. Sometimes a bucktail cast across the current and retrieved in a skittering manner will arouse bass; often a smallmouth will follow the bucktail all the way across the river, taking it just when your retrieve stops.

I have also had remarkable fishing at times in fast rivers by letting a streamer fly drift with the current on a long slack line, getting it down into white water directly below me, then retrieving with the rod held high above my head and making the fly bounce from one rip to the next.

This is a particularly good method to try in shallow, broken areas where there is no evidence of holding water. Lightly dressed streamers such as the Black Ghost are ideal for this type of fishing. And don't neglect trying tiny feather streamers tied on #10 and #12 long-shank hooks. These "baby" minnows are especially popular on Eastern streams right now for low, clear water conditions.

In lake fishing, the streamer fly is most difficult to use properly. Here there is no helpful current to animate the feathers. Most anglers try to reach out as far as possible, then, by stripping the line in even pulls, bring the lure back minnow-fashion. That is easy. But for the most part it is not wholly effective. The fly should sink deep and be retrieved erratically, fast and slow, in long pulls and short, as well as worked at the surface in mechanical jerks. The expert streamer fisherman will bring the fly back in various depths and speeds with each cast.

In a great many cases the trolled streamer fly is more effective than one that is cast. This is particularly true of coho, chinook, and landlocked salmon fishing. Although a trolling action is contrary to general streamer practice, the trolled fly is a steadily moving form, one that may in a short area simulate the flight of a smelt or needlefish. The important point is that the fly is constantly moving and without hesitation for a long distance (something which you could not accomplish when casting) and salmon often follow a fly for long distances before finally taking. In effect, trolling keeps the angler moving away from his quarry, the far-off disturbance of the canoe having little significance, whereas a follow-up to the side of a stationary canoe exposes the angler and his rod. (The indifference of salmon and squaretails toward boat noises is so extreme that it is a common practice to troll in the wake of an outboard, catching fish on a trolled streamer a few yards astern.)

There are streamer flies tied specially for trolling, incidentally, but they are used almost exclusively in Maine and the Pacific Northwest. The trolling streamer gets a big play among landlocked salmon and coho salmon anglers. It consists of two hooks tied in tandem (these are joined by means of nylon, wire, or bead chain) and this construction serves a dual purpose: it permits the tying of a long, slim fly that more closely simulates smelt, candlefish, and herring where a single hook would be completely over-dressed; and the extra hook gets any short-striking fish. Such flies cannot be cast successfully because the wing gets fouled up with the hooks. But under the conditions for which they are designed, trolling streamers are better than regular-length streamer flies.

I think one of the most telling additions to my streamer fly work was the use of marabou flies. We never got around to using them until just before I left the Delaware country, and I think if Dan had known about them earlier, we would have taken most of those cannibals we had to get with live bait. We were fishing one of the big pools above Harvard one morning when Dan spotted a nice smallmouth in a pocket where the stream splits. The fish held against an undercut bank behind a pile of brush. It was Dan's claim, so I sat on a stump and watched. He made three bad casts but the bass didn't see them. The fourth cast clunked the water hard right over the fish, but no sooner had the bass ducked for cover than the marabou began working and the smallmouth wheeled right out again. The old bass followed the fly for a few feet, then slipped back toward the bank. The next few casts were good ones, with the streamer drifting back to the fish, and each time the smallmouth followed the marabou back upstream, getting more and more excited. Finally, Dan put one more cast in that pocket and retrieved it real slow; and when the marabou reached the brush where Dan couldn't get any more line, the bass ripped into the fly. Over the ensuing forty years, the fatal fascination of marabou streamers has become well known, and marabou—either by itself or adapted to a Muddler-type pattern—probably now accounts for more really big trout than any other streamer design.

Clinic

No single streamer pattern had a greater impact on fly fishing than the Muddler Minnow beginning in the 1950s. A departure from what was considered orthodox streamer design, Don Gapen's innovation of a fat deerhair head to imitate the sculpin has spawned countless Muddler-type flies with that key feature. But regardless of pattern, streamer flies are at their best early in the spring season, and again in the fall, and at any time at dusk or after a rain when the water is slightly discolored and a showy fly is needed. In small, clear water streams, dressings on #6 to #10 hooks are most effective, but in heavy water, particularly on Western rivers, big #2 to #1/0 patterns are popular.

Beginning anglers experience a lot of missed strikes with streamer flies due to improper line control. As mentioned in this chapter, the rod tip must be held *low* to minimize slack and to tighten quickly when a fish hits. The rod should never be at an angle higher than parallel to the surface, and preferably the tip should be almost touching the water. A floating-type fly line is preferable to a sinking line since it's easier to control and lift out of the water; however, when rivers are running bank-full in the spring season, it will probably be necessary to compromise and use a sinking-tip line to get the fly down to trout level.

8

THINK SMALL

Arnold Gingrich observed in *The Joys of Trout* (Crown, 1973) that "fly-fishing is the most fun you can have standing up." Well, frustration is not unknown in any position. I once watched a young lady in a tearful tantrum splinter a bamboo rod over her knee and throw it in the Beaverkill. Judging by the way she limped, it was a Uslan five-strip. For that matter, my boyhood hero, Babe Ruth, threw *his* rod in the Esopus, then inexplicably jumped into the river from the Phoenicia bridge—an explosion that probably registered on a seismograph. However, the Sultan of Swat was known to bend an elbow on occasion, which probably clouded his resolve. I've never reached the rod-breaking stage but I must admit, there have been times when the brown trout tempted me.

I arrived at Manhattan Spring Creek, in Montana, on a day when the air sings like a chiming crystal, while high in the distance a new powder of snow sparkled like diamond dust on mountain peaks—and the sun shed a dulcet radiance on a fantastic *Tricorythodes* hatch that had every trout in the stream greedily slurping and sipping on the surface. Ah, but where was my fancy Wheatly fly box, chock full of #22s and #24s that a trico hatch requires? Why, in my duffle bag 40 miles yonder in the motel. My feeble reasoning that something entirely different from the abundant naturals would attract a few charitable fish produced two suicidal rainbows on a #16 Adams, while big browns dimpled all around me. The rest of the day was spent shuffling patterns like a monkey going through his routine to earn a banana. I even tried scissoring the Adams down but it still looked like a tugboat, drifting among mayflies with a body length of one-tenth inch. A couple of fish hit a barrel knot in my leader, which is about the size of a trico natural. Selectively rising brown trout always remind me of an oligarchy of Harvard professors in Harris tweeds, holding a seminar on The Theory of Probability and Statistics. If a naked blonde wiggled through the room carrying a sign reading DOWN WITH TRICOS, nobody would change the subject.

The brown trout can be absolutely mind-blowing when feeding rhythmically in the surface film for almost invisible insects (a phenomenon historically known as "the angler's curse"), as it must ingest two or three thousand tricos to pass a good burp, while loftier foods float by unmolested. The rainbow will act this way at times, and so to a lesser extent will the cutthroat and on rare occasions the brook trout. *Salmo trutta* is the thinking man's trout, at least in its fluvial form, as we often wait in groveling attendance for the privilege of being sneered at. Undeniably, those fabled "super" hatches, such as the Green Drake, Giant Salmon Fly, Hendrickson, and Michigan Caddis, are totally classic in content; the emergences are big, the rising fish often the biggest, and the imitative patterns highly visible at #10 up to #6. However, these stirring episodes are brief in duration, with perhaps a few days or a week of activity. In 1983, the Giant Salmon Fly hatch was a washout due to a fast-melting snowpack that flooded many Western rivers. Fortunately, other hatches of regional importance occur intermittently during the season: the Blue-Winged Olive, March Brown, Green Caddis, Quill Gordon, Brown Drake, Pale Evening Dun, Light Cahill, ad infinitum. By contrast, and despite their diminutive size, the Tricorythidae and Caenidae families of mayflies are choice trout foods throughout the United States, with a long period of emergence from June through October. On quality alkaline streams these hatches can't be avoided. In addition, other minutiae such as the chironomids or midges (which hatch right through the winter), numerous caddisflies (especially the tiny Hydroptilidae), and many species of beetles and ants will trigger a feeding orgy as enigmatic as the feast of Belshazzar. Collectively, these "micros," which are fly sizes in the 20s, are the key to some splendid fishing.

In the innocent age when we still thought the angling world was flat (I believed it began and ended with the Delaware & Ulster Railroad) and patterns like the Grizzly King and Wickham's Fancy were still in Catskill currency, I don't ever recall using a fly smaller than a #16, because we didn't have synthetic leaders in those days. A .005-inch silkworm gut was the finest diameter available. It wouldn't hold a geriatric bluegill. Today, and it seems like a minor miracle in retrospect, we can fish with dressings down to #28 on .003-inch nylon at 8X testing three-quarters of a pound and with enough elasticity to absorb the shocks of hooking and playing modest-sized trout. This is not the kind of tippet you are going to throw in Lake Pedder, where those lacustrine browns are as dangerous as the local Tasmanian tiger snakes, and a #2/0 Mudeye is a mere hors d'oeuvre for 12- to 20-pound fish. However, on the Yellow Breeches, Au Sable, or North Platte, where trout are proudly described in inches, modern fleaweight tackle is an ultimate weapon.

The New Fork River in Wyoming is one of those merry streams that plunges and splashes into a willow bank, then sweeps in a long curve into another bank before dancing away in long riffles that drop into deep cliff-bordered pools. It is quality water with a good population of 12- to 20-inch brown trout. I've had memorable days on this river with Jimmy Green and Larry Madison making daily scores of more than 50 releases on the dry fly. There are some slow stretches that generate terrific hatches and in one of these Jimmy and I saw what had to be a 10-pound brown with a tail like a shovel (at a distance we mistook it for a beaver) gulping clots of tricos after a spinner fall. It was in this same stretch that I caught the best trout I've ever taken on a #20. This occurred during a midge emergence when the browns were on top, rolling in head and tail rises for pupae suspended in the surface film.

We were float boating that day and at noon Ted Trueblood and I pulled out to wait for Jimmy and Phil Clock to catch up. I had been rowing the double-ender all morning, so while Ted gathered firewood I waded below our lunch site. Trout were popping everywhere. I was rigged for fast water with a big hairwing, which didn't interest these fish. They just kept rising all around it. I saw some midges beginning to swarm but there were probably a million pupae in the surface for every adult taking flight. With shaking fingers, I took about ten minutes to retaper my leader. My prize was feeding in midstream. I dropped an Olive Midge a few feet above his station four or five times before the leader showed a little pull and was fast to a brown that evidently had a bonefish ancestor. The trout bolted downstream, well into my backing, while I ran behind shouting for Ted to bring a landing net.

I never pressure a strong-running fish on a gossamer tippet. At such times I point my rod horizontally and play the trout off the reel against the click, counting on the friction of the line running through the water to slow the fish down. This doesn't allow any control if the fish decides to dive in a weed bed or under a stump but using the full bend of the rod results in too many snapped tippets. My fish came to the surface, wallowing and threshing, and I finally managed to gentle him into a quiet backwater. At which point, I skidded down a clay bank and sat in the New Fork.

"Well that was pretty fancy, what else can you do?" I looked up and there was grinning Trueblood with the net. The fish circled slowly at my feet. It was the most fun I could have sitting down. New Fork trout are handsome fish, more gold than brown, and this heavily spotted male taped 22 inches. The best I've ever taken on 6X, with a #20 fly.

My favorite rod for fishing with micros is the 7½-foot, 2½-ounce Paul Young Perfectionist calibered for a 4-weight line. There are other bamboos just as suitable, but what I want is a rod with a slow casting cycle, so I can "paint" the fly on target. The current preoccupation with speed-of-recovery in space age materials, boron and graphite, is in one sense misleading; it's fabulous when you need to get a fly out fast in front of a cruising tarpon, or bang a Polar Shrimp at a far-off steelhead, but when trout are rising in pockets of silky water between weed sweepers, the *last* thing I want in a rod is speed. Teacup accuracy with a controlled turnover at distances up to 40 feet is much more realistic. Instead of a double taper, which is superior to a weight-forward for micro fishing, I've switched to the new Lee Wulff triangle taper in his 4–5 weight (this runs progressively from .030 to .055 inches in 40 feet, then drops to a .032-inch shooting line for 90 feet). This puts the finest line near the fish at normally effective distances, while providing the weight for long casts when needed. I wouldn't advise a line heavier than a 6-weight. A heavy taper contributes to broken tippets simply because it has to be pulled with more force to overcome surface tension when setting the hook. You can reflexively wallop a trout with 2X or 3X but micro tippets don't permit much more than a tightening of the line. The fly is so small that a trout won't reject it instantly, as it would with larger artificials, so the speed of response is not critical. Fish will occasionally slurp a micro and swim down with it, literally hooking themselves.

To get a drag-free drift with micros, a long leader is essential, no less than 9 feet and preferably 12 feet in length. My own leader formula for all trout fishing is 60 percent *hard* monofilament in the heavy diameters—i.e., the butt and two or three step-down strands—and the balance soft monofilament. While hard monofilament smoothly transmits energy from the line in the turnover, it's too rigid for a lifelike drift with small flies, and especially with tiny micros. In addition, it's easier to cast slack in the leader with soft monofilament, thereby delaying drag which is almost invisible to the human eye when you are fishing with #20s or smaller. For this reason I prefer a long tippet, never less than 28 inches, and usually 36 inches when using 5X to 8X. Bear in mind that the longer the tippet, the greater its elasticity. If you don't tie your own leaders you can find the hard/soft combination in several mail-order catalogs (I can't vouch for their tapers, but firms like Orvis, Dan Bailey, and Cortland purvey quality products).

One of the most beautiful stretches of brown trout water in the West is that 20-mile leg of the upper Madison that lies within Yellowstone Park. There are places on the lower Madison that produce more and bigger fish but, after mid-September, when the park traffic becomes a trickle, the lodgepole-pine-clad run with its elk meadows spangled in luminous frost is worth the detour. Much of the stream bottom here consists of slopes and holes camouflaged by stonewort and milfoil weed, making it rather tricky to wade. The compelling urge to fish it is, I suppose, for the same masochistic reason Charley Ritz used to rave about another trout stream (which the upper Madison is), the Andelle in France, where a pair of 10-inch trout was cause for celebration. I've had my best luck below Madison Junction with sunk patterns, especially dragonfly nymphs and attractors like the Black Wooly Bugger. On my last visit,

with my daughter Susan, the water was dead as the proverbial doornail; we took two 15-inch browns on the Bugger
and had less luck at nightfall with soggy French fries and
rubbery T-bones, which I am convinced are as endemic
to Montana's restaurants as the Giant Salmon Fly is to its
rivers.

At pink dawn the next day, which was the end of our
annual roving vacation together, we decided to give the
upper Madison one more chance, if just to gawk at the
bears, elk, and moose that were in greater evidence than
the trout. We arrived in a blizzard of tricos. Susan hooked
the first fish while I was still trying to form a double turle
knot behind the eye of a black Poly-Wing Spinner. This has
become the universal pattern for a trico with its long white
tail, white wings, and black body. I have a hell of a time
knotting a #24 on 7X, even with granny glasses, and,
come dusk, old Dad can't even find the fly between thumb
and forefinger with any frequency. I rarely venture to the
ultimate #28, which must be dressed by a myopic lapidary.
When hook sizes are numbered in the 20s I much prefer
turned-up eyes, rather than turned-down, as the rake or
direction of penetration with a turned-up eye is downward,
and it provides the maximum gape between eye and hook
point. This requires a dual purpose knot, providing reasonable strength with minimum bulk, while allowing the
hook to be pulled in a straight line, thus tipping the point
down on contact. The bulk of the knot should be secured
behind the eye and not in front of it, and for this purpose
it's hard to beat the double turle. If a knot is formed in
front of the eye, a tiny hook will articulate and the fly will
skim nose down over the surface. There are marginally
stronger knots than the double turle but none that I know
of is better suited to fishing micros.

Within an hour spent spinners fell to the water and
trout were swirling all over the stream. No matter where we

banked, stalked, or waded there would be a half dozen fish within casting range. Most of the bigger trout were stationed between weed sweepers, gulping clots of dead insects, often requiring eight or ten casts to get the Poly-Wing in the right spot at the critical open-mouth instant. Some of our fish broke off in the botanicals, including one that would probably go 3 pounds. With so much activity we didn't bother to eat lunch. By three in the afternoon, the river was silent again. The Madison's generosity had clearly run out. I don't recall another *Tricorythodes* hatch that lasted that many hours.

The brown is undeniably the most challenging of all trout no matter where it is found, and while effective techniques run the whole spectrum of angling disciplines, at times it pays to think small. Indeed, you will have no choice.

Clinic

The double turle knot is compact, and, equally important, when you use it your leader tippet will come out straight through the eye of the fly. This serves the opposite purpose from a loop knot (as described in chapter 2); the double turle will *prevent* articulation.

With any knots (such as the popular improved clinch knot) of the types that are jammed in front of a turned-up hook eye, the fly will sooner or later "cock" at an obtuse

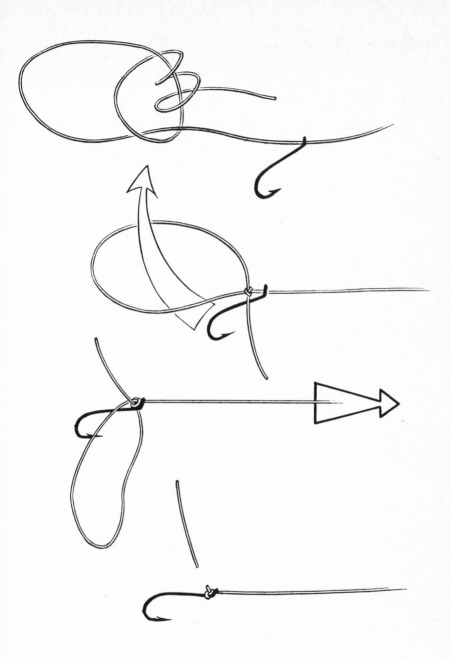

Double turle knot

angle due to casting impetus. If you're using a tiny micro, this may leave your fly standing on its nose, or submerged tail down, in a most unlifelike manner. With the double turle this won't happen.

To tie the double turle, first pass the tippet through the eye, then slide the fly down the leader out of the way and form a double slip knot in the tag end; draw this closed, forming a loop. Slide the fly back up to the knot and pass it upward through the loop, so the loop is now below the fly and the knot behind the eye. Grasp the standing part of the tippet and pull to tighten. Clip off the tag end. The double turle is also the most traditional knot for large salmon flies.

9

STALKING THE BONEFISH

Wading and stalking bonefish is not everybody's cup of tea, but to me it's the ultimate method. It does require flats with a firm substrate, preferably white sand with a minimum of grass, which is one reason why I favor fishing in the Bahamas. We do have some good flats in Florida, but for every solid-to-the-foot mile here, there are probably 10 miles in the islands. The great sand bank at Ambergris Cay, the Joulters, Deadman's Cay, Santa Maria Point, French Wells, and the many locations near Deep Water Cay such as Big Mangrove, Big Harbour, Jacob's Cay, Brush Cay, the Bird Bar, and East End Creek come to mind just as favorite salmon pools stir old memories. The advantage of wading and, indeed, the real thrill, is that you can get much closer to the fish. And you can also take them in the shallowest water where a skiff would go aground. Tailing incomers will sometimes swim within 10 feet before spooking provided you get down on your knees. In a sense, it is comparable to the matador's classic *pase de rodillas* (literally a pass at the bull made while kneeling) as the fish almost blindly charges the fly. In the bonefish's cone of vision there is a vast difference between an angler standing on a bow platform looming 8 or 9 feet above the surface and the angler who kneels in the water. Incomers will often swim so close that you will get splashed at the strike, provided your derriere is flat against your heels. Politely bending at the waist or crouching is little better than standing upright in critical eyeball-to-eyeball encounters. Unfortunately, stalked fish are not always incomers, and you have to play "catch up" or go looking for another target.

I have followed big bonefish over a quarter mile of flat, loners that seemed to sense that outer limit where a cast is impossible, yet pausing to tail just often enough to make the stalk compelling. This often ends with the fish being spooked by a shark or the shadow of a passing gull. Or by a very poor presentation on my part because I'm pumped full of adrenaline and staggering in marl.

I can still see Fred Cushing stalking his first bonefish. It had been a miserable day with gusting northwesterly winds and running schools, and now with the sun almost on the horizon and the tide ebbing fast, fish began tailing among the mangrove shoots. These were quick feeders; first they would stand on their heads and then, before you could get within casting range, their tails would vanish and the fish would move another 10 feet to tail again. Fred waded cautiously behind, dragging his shooting line on the surface as they grubbed across a shallow bank. Each time he stopped to make a cast, the fish ducked under and swam off, staying just out of casting range. The hard sand bottom shelved into soft marl, and Fred began wobbling like a drunk who had one foot stuck in the cuspidor. Finally, almost at the end of the bank, the bonefish raised its caudal fin in the air as Fred closed the gap to about 50 feet. He made a fast haul and just as the rod curved to full bend a bananaquit, that ubiquitous Bahaman warbler, probably weary of bucking the wind and mistaking it for a mangrove shoot—flitted down and perched on the bonefish's tail. The reaction on the part of all three participants was instantaneous. The fish busted a hole in the surface, rocketing away so fast that the bird was left standing in space while the ordinarily unflappable Mr. Cushing shouted "Oh!" and slammed his rod on the water. But frustration is the name of the game. It's worse than golf, which is why Jack Nicklaus bought a home on Great Harbour Cay.

Some years ago, Jim Chapralis, who does that almost biblical monthly newsletter the *PanAngler,* and I were wading that great white flat at Ambergris Cay. Jim is a fine caster, having won two international tournaments, and immediately after meeting some tailing fish we were hooked up. It looked like it was going to be a good day. Jim was about 100 yards away and working parallel to me, which is a sensible tactic as often one angler can spot fish swimming in the direction of the other and signal their approach. A few fish later the wind began picking up, and instead of tails we were faced with schools pushing big wakes as they came down the flat. These were no ordinary schools but a hundred or more fish in a tight formation that would run in one direction, then nervously break left and right. Sometimes this can be productive if you lay the fly out 40 or 50 feet ahead of the fish and are lucky enough to have them swim into it; big running schools are not easy.

I double hauled with the wind and dropped the fly way ahead of one school. They passed by it, over it, and around

it. My floating line was left rocking in their wake. By stripping in fast I still had another chance as the fish veered to
my left. I made a perfect shot at nothing. The school
wheeled in the opposite direction and went to my right. I
botched the next cast by forgetting to compensate for what
was now a crosswind. The fly plopped right in the middle
of them, which sent the fish running toward Jim. He was
already in a half crouch, flailing at another school. A veritable silvery horde came funneling from left again, and for
a few seconds I watched Chapralis do an adagio dance. I
thought he'd rip his pants as he threw line all around the
compass trying to intercept a target. The flat was just one
mass of milling fish—now actually spooking each other.
They were not even looking at our feathers. At one point
Jim stood there with the fly line draped over his ears while
a few hundred bonefish charged past his legs. It looked as
if he had stepped on a land mine. I made one more cast that
plucked a scale from the back of a fish who swam into the
fly accidentally.

The phenomenon of running schools is not easy to
understand and less explicable than a plague of bullfrogs.
It may be the stage of the tide, the intensity of the wind,
even the presence of an unseen predator, or a combination
of these factors that keeps the fish moving. Instead of
booming off the flat at top speed, the way a spooked bone
usually departs, the fish often wheel in aimless circles. I
think that this behavior, which often happens on the ebb
tide, is an attempt at recruitment—when small pods of fish
that have been feeding since the flood gather in a school
and one group seeks another large unit before heading
toward deep water. Essentially, the activities of all school-
oriented fish are integrated. They turn right or left, maintaining a precise distance from each other, and travel at
identical speeds. This pattern starts in early life when fish
of equal size join a group whose speed and responses to

maneuvering are the same. When feeding they may scatter to some extent, but if panicked they react by coming together again in the synchronized movement of a unit rather than that of a group of individuals. The only protection a bonefish has, and it must be a small comfort, is numerical abundance. Despite its very considerable speed, both sharks and barracuda often wait in ambush and at times will nail a bonefish dead in its tracks.

David Wayne and I once ran into a school of bonefish of the East End flat that easily contained a thousand fish. They came downtide toward our skiff, surging around us, then circling and coming back looking like a dark cloud against the white sand. We cast to them, of course, but their panicky behavior suggested that something was wrong. Then we spotted four big lemon sharks blocking their exit on the only deep side of the flat and another pair herding them in the shallows. The bottom topography was not favorable for escape at that tidal stage, and when the school finally flushed at tremendous speed, there was a brief series of explosions with one shark taking a bonefish in the air. On another occasion while fishing a narrow bay in the Middle Bight at Andros, I saw a pack of big barracuda chase a school of bonefish out of the water. About a dozen fish literally leaped on the beach. Bonefish inevitably find themselves in culs-de-sac when lingering too long in a lush feeding pasture and, for their survival in this predatory world, Nature has created one of the spookiest fish in the sea. Ted Williams calls them "nervous wrecks," which may well describe my own state of mind at times. As Ted observed, "You can scare bonefish by sneezing. You can spook a whole school by clearing your throat or scraping your rod on the gunwale of your boat. I've raised my voice at somebody's lousy cast and cleaned off an entire flat."

Wading and stalking is a very personal experience, a

one-on-one contest. Some years ago, a friend of mine,
Norman Castle, whose sporting preference runs to open
ocean power-boat racing where people go dashing around
at 160 miles an hour suffering a considerable mortality
rate, asked if he could spend a day with me on the flats.
"I don't want to fish," said Norman, "I just want to see
what it's all about." It turned out to be a day when the
nearby flats at Chub Cay were absolutely barren, so we
motored that serpentine right branch of Airport Creek into
a mangrove lake. I had a hunch the extreme spring tide was
delivering schools well inland. This lake is a botanical
nightmare with only a few areas of open water more than
100 yards in width. It's a broad patchwork of shoots and
bushes. Norman sat in the stern puffing on his pipe while
Austin Pinder poled. I spotted a school of maybe a dozen
smallish fish working a turtle-grass bed, but beyond them,

tailing in the opposite direction, was a single of about 8 or 9 pounds moving slowly among the mangroves. It was obvious that if I spooked the school the solo feeder would bolt.

I eased out of the skiff planning a semicircular stalk that would take me around intervening bushes using as much screen as possible, and hoping that the single would follow his present course. Here and there I stepped into some soft bottom and spent precious seconds trying to quietly ease my feet out of the marl. Finally, with Polaroids fogged by sweat, I peeked around a mangrove and there was my fish, raising tail, sparkling silver in the sun. I usually come apart at the seams at this stage in a stalk. It's like buck fever, and the years haven't noticeably diminished that emotion. The sun was overhead so I wasn't concerned with throwing a line flash or shadow so much as clearing the mangroves on my backcast.

The fly dropped a few feet ahead of the fish, who halted abruptly as though puzzled by its entry, then swam over and swallowed it. This began one of the most exhausting twenty minutes of play I can ever recall. No matter which direction the fish took, my line was around mangrove shoots and branches. I wallowed like a water buffalo clearing the line, while trying to put pressure on an absolutely berserk fish that was alternately dashing through open parts of the lake, then running around another bush. My leg muscles were so cramped that twice I fell to my knees. Little of this was visible to Norman until my fish came through an opening that led back to the skiff with me charging behind. Fortunately, Austin is quick with the net. Wiping gobs of marl off my face and shirt, I was puffing so hard I couldn't even speak. Norman sat in his cloud of pipe smoke looking more puzzled than congratulatory.

Then he asked quite innocently, "Is *that* all there is to it?"

Many people hesitate to wade because of the occasional presence of sharks, barracuda, and rays. I would never "expert" anybody on the subject except to acknowledge the potential danger. I am not about to get in the water if a big hammerhead is cruising the flat, or a pod of lemons or blacktips are obviously on patrol. However, wading is most productive below knee depth and often ankle deep, which is not enough water to float a big predator. I must admit that I've felt uneasy at times when wading a long distance from the skiff, then crossing an unexpected channel at hip depth only to meet an overly curious barracuda. Rays are not aggressive, and if you shuffle your feet along the bottom there is no chance of stepping on one. (I would not say the same thing about the freshwater rays that pose a real danger in tropical South American rivers.)

Wading the flats without protective foot gear and a pair of slacks invites some problems. Broken shells, sea urchins and coral can deliver painful wounds to bare feet. While these can normally be avoided, one's focus in sighting fish is at a distance rather than underfoot, and once the stalk begins your total concentration should be on the moving target. Studying the bottom for even a few seconds is time enough for a fish to completely change direction and be lost in the surface glare. Thick-rubber-soled Topsiders are ideal protection. With these I wear light, tight-fitting wool socks to prevent abrasion from the sand and bits of shell that gradually collect inside the shoe. Slacks offer additional protection from long-spined urchins, standing corals, and the rare contact with jellyfishes; both the stinging nettle jellyfish (*Chrysaora quinquecirrha*) and the cubomedusa or "sea wasp" (*Chiropsalmus quadrumanus*) may occur in shallow water. Only once in many years of wading the flats have I encountered the sea wasp, and on that occasion I was wearing bathing trunks. The pain was unforgettable. Nettle jellyfish with their pale white bells ribbed with reddish markings are easily seen, but the little sea wasp has a completely transparent bell and is virtually invisible until powerful stinging cells announce their presence. Slacks also provide protection against sunburn, which is a constant threat whether one wades or not.

Many years ago, I rounded the bend in Big Harbour Creek and passed an anchored skiff in the middle of the channel. There was a man seated in the bow, one amidships who was evidently dunking a bait with a spinning rod, and another in the stern. Bow and stern looked like two Chicago hoodlums, and all three were attired in black overcoats with felt fedoras pulled over their ears. Curt Gowdy had just arrived at camp to do an "American Sportsman" TV segment.

"What are you doing, Curt, a fashion show?"

"Oh, that's Prince Rainier and his bodyguards. They're afraid of getting sunburned."

I suppose that was the ultimate protection from ultraviolet rays at that time, but today sunscreen lotions are more effective because you won't collapse from heat stroke. Sunscreens are labeled with an SPF (sun protection factor) rating to indicate how many hours would equal one hour of no protection. In other words, a rating of SPF 8 means it will take eight hours of exposure to equal one unprotected hour without a sunscreen. But SPF ratings range from 4 to as high as 15. Although sunscreens are *not* tanning lotions, you will still develop some color as only the skin-damaging ultraviolet rays (or UVB's) are blocked out and not the wavelengths that create a tan (or UVA's). My nose and lips are particularly sensitive, so I also carry a stick of protective sunscreen (Avon Sun Seekers SPF 15) that fits handily in my shirt pocket and can be wiped on between bouts with the bonefish.

Clinic

Ultrasonic tracking of transmitter-equipped bonefish in 1980 and 1981 at Deep Water Cay, Bahamas, indicated that schools follow a regular "path" when entering and leaving a flat, according to the bottom topography. Knowing where to intercept fish as the water floods, or ebbs, is, of course, one of the skills of experienced bonefish guides. Once on the flat and actively feeding, a school usually disperses into pods and singles and the pattern of their movement becomes more random in the search for food. This is the most productive time to stalk bonefish by wading before the water reaches flood stage.

Tailers in ankle- to knee-deep water can be approached very closely; some fish may work away from you,

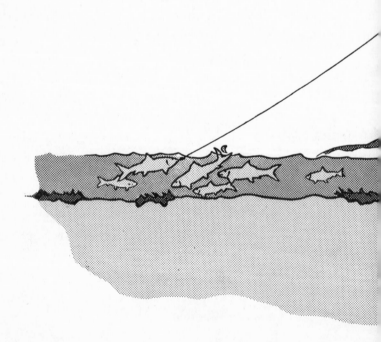

but ideally there will be some "incomers." When wading, I keep about 10 feet of line extended from the rod and trailing in the water, and about 25 feet of line in loose coils in my other hand. Making as little disturbance as possible by shuffling my feet along the bottom, I can usually get within 30 feet of the fish before getting down on my knees and casting. From this position, even if the fish turn on an incoming path, it's possible to make more than one presentation. In very thin water the dry fly can be quite effective.

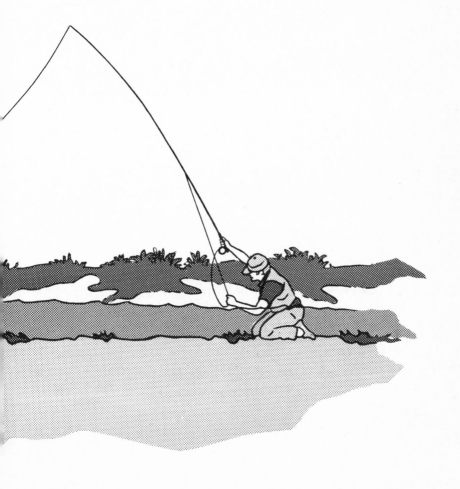

10

STEELHEAD SUMMER

Jackson Ames said that Mahah, the evil Indian spirit, was on the east side of the river, but that devil steelhead came out of the sunrise threshing water in an end-over-end pinwheel run and a rod-throbbing step of a brush dance. For three days Jackson Ames beat the bottom of his boat with a stick to get Mahah out of the hull. His friend Jimmy Jaynes did a Brodie in the Lower Lamm Riffle, and nobody could find Jimmy. That was Mahah. Mahah could get in a boat and he could get in the river, but now the evil Yurok spirit was gone.

In the algae-green Klamath, a 200-mile-long vein of the Pacific, Jim Nelson and I caught 16 steelhead that morning, and when the screws fell out of my reel frame we went back to camp and busted our alarm clock to get new ones. We both caught 6 more steelhead, and when Jim's reel fell apart I had what was left of the alarm clock in the belly pouch of my waders, so we didn't waste time going back to the tent. There were more steelhead in Johnson's Riffle and more in Mettah Riffle, and by dark we were repairing our reels with copper paper clips. That's the way it is when the evil spirit has gone from the river. You don't need an alarm clock.

Some riffle regulars may remember the year 1945 as a bell-ringer on coastal streams. Catching steelhead was like playing the hammer game in a Chicago stockyard. A gent could step into the Klamath, for instance, and maul a dozen big summer fish, and if he had the strength to throw a golf ball over the post office he could stand in one spot and bang fish all day. But the runs are not always so thick that wee tots and old ladies can cold-deck 8- and 10-pound steelies. Between abundance and scarcity rests the lore of fly fishing. In good years, all water is holding water and short casts are the rule rather than the exception. But in slow years, one must prospect the water carefully and learn about his quarry all over again.

The day Jim Nelson and I parlayed our steelhead vendetta into a hassle of historic proportions was preceded by several days of dull fishing. In fact, we felt lucky to check out with one or two good fish. An upriver Yurok told us that he had seen trout wallowing in a certain riffle the night before, so we simply worked upstream until we found the main school. Summer runs throb out of the ocean like shots of electricity and you never know where they will ground. But the interesting fact, which we put to use, was that these fish were holding at the break in the tail of a long riffle. They rested in relatively the same place in three riffles above. You could fish miles of normally productive water without even turning a half-pounder, but if you skimmed a fly in the oily-looking slick just before the current started to bounce again, you could tab five or six fish. I caught seven in an area of no more than 10 square yards. Grandpa Hoecorn said we were chasing squaws through the huckleberries, but with a hundred rods waving on Blake's Riffle, our discovery was as welcome as a fresh breath from the smokehouse.

Steelhead fishing is primarily wet-fly fishing. There are occasions when the fish will come to a dry fly, but in coastal rivers, floating a fly is hard work and the water has to be clear so that you know you're covering fish. The Deschutes stonefly (salmon fly) hatch, or the salmon fly hatch on the North Umpqua, will sometimes bring enough big rainbows to the surface to make dry-fly casting feasible, but the elementary approach is still a quartering cross-stream swing with the fly drifting sunk. It is not always necessary to cast long distances; in fact, many fine fish are hooked within a 30-foot radius. Given the right wind, one has the tendency to cast far beyond holding water. Casting should be done in a series of drops by facing cross-stream, making short probes first and then longer ones, until you've covered all the likely spots within range. Then wade a few steps downstream and repeat the procedure, allowing each cast to swing around and straighten in the current before retrieving.

Except for classic rivers like the North Umpqua in Oregon, or the Stamp in British Columbia, where the character of the streambed provides holds along ledges and submerged boulders, nearly all fly fishing is done in long riffles, the bouncy water running between pools. On the North Umpqua, especially in that area from Steamboat Creek down to the Big Canyon, through Mott Pool, Kitchen Pool, and Rock Creek, and on the Stamp River from the mouth of the Ash through Money Pool and the

Black Rock, there are miles of swirling, glassy-clear stream where the trout hold along gravelbars, behind rocks, or whatever else is handy. Winter-run fish, however, are inclined to favor slow water, and many of them are taken on the bottoms of pools with weighted flies such as the Optic bucktails popularized by the late Jim Pray on the Eel River. But the steelheader is largely a "riffle bird," casting and drifting his fly in quarter circles as he wades downstream.

There are several schools of thought concerning the choice of fly pattern for steelhead. In general, any standard dressing, such as the Umpqua, Thor, Cumming's Special, Carson, Golden Demon, Polar Shrimp, or Gray Hackle Yellow, will produce fish on #4 and #6 hooks. I once, through several weeks of continuous fishing, used nothing but a Burlap fly tied on a #4 hook, and when the steelies shredded it almost to the bare hook, I simply put on a fresh one. Pop Morris summed this up one night when he was snaffling one big fish after another on Blue Creek Riffle. A city sport asked Pop what fly the steelhead were taking, and Pop replied, "I dunno what they're taking, but I've been giving 'em a Gray Hackle for sixty years."

A few riffles upstream from Pop's stand were two operators who really cut the mustard: Mrs. Hick Kelsey, who tied and flipped nothing but a Brown Hackle with red tag, and Bert Best, who confined himself to the Gray Hackle with an orange tail. Pop once had a passion for the Thor tied upside down. His idea was that the fish are hooked in the roof of the mouth, which prods them into a better fight. If Pop had found somebody who tied Gray Hackles upside down, he probably would have ignored the Thor.

The critical school of casters, as represented by author Claude Kreider, favors dark or dull-colored patterns for upriver and clear water fishing, and flashy attractors for downriver or murky-water fishing. Mr. Kreider also made some attempt at insect imitation and reputedly earned considerable poundage during the days of hatching insects. Roderick L. Haig-Brown, the late guiding light of the British Columbia streams, was likewise both imitator and impressionist, running the gamut from nymph to salmon fly representations. The gaily colored General Money flies are held in high esteem from Vancouver north, and, for the most part, a swatch of bright orange or red can be found in most patterns.

I think it's important that a steelhead wet fly be sparsely dressed on heavy wire hooks. The correct amount of material can be seen in flies that were tied by Wes Drain, Mike Kennedy, Jim Nelson, Don Harger, or Roy Donnelly.

When steelhead come upriver they let you know about it; there's a banging and a splashing from rolling fish. They often hold in a group rather than spread out over a riffle, and this is most apparent among fresh-run fish in the lower 10 or 12 miles, evidently because of their schooling habits prior to actual migration. I waded the length of Johnson's Riffle on the Klamath late one afternoon without getting a bump. I worked over the break and down into Lower Johnson Riffle, through the head and halfway down to the tail before hitting that one inexplicable spot.

There was no water sign—haystack, slick, bounce, or gravelbar—but a bright fish rose and took the fly in a turn and ran directly upstream before jumping. Then he jumped four times, high, clean, and kicking, before he threw the hook. I recovered line and wits quick enough to get another drift over the same spot, and a second steelhead hit. After a violent series of twisting jumps and fifteen minutes of maneuvering, I led a 6-pounder into quiet water. The fish had taken me some distance below the hold, so I walked back, waded out, and hooked another one in exactly the same place. They were small fish, not more than two or three days out of the Pacific and full of vinegar. I hooked eight and landed five.

It is a cardinal rule of lower-river fishing always to work the same spot until you know that you've cleaned house, because that might very well be all the action you will get. That's the way the ball bounces. Jim and I got into a hot spot on the lower Rogue one day where the single-eggers couldn't hold their drift boats. One double-ender had so many sports on board that it looked like a Chinese gunboat having a fire drill. The braintruster who was running this craft dragged anchor as far as the slick, but the Rogue is too much river and away they went over the break. We clobbered trout after trout in that one place, even though the egg addicts were shuttling back and forth over the hold.

When the runs get 20 or 30 miles upriver, or when the fish have been in fresh water for a few weeks, the steelhead reverts to his old rainbow habit, and this is when finesse, fine leaders, and small dark flies begin to pay off. Now there is less grouping and milling around. A careless Klamath River fish is usually spooky and nervous by the time he reaches Happy Camp on the upper river; if he slides into the jade-green waters of the Trinity, you might find him a loner and a gourmet. You can make the banjo ring with bright flies upriver, but for day-in and day-out casting I'd favor patterns that are predominantly gray or black, like the Black Gnat or Witch. Of course, there is a greater possibility of taking steelhead on the dry fly in upriver pools, and regular trout patterns down to #10 dressings are effective.

Selecting the proper line for steelhead fishing should be predicated on the idea that you will have to cast 60 or 70 feet, usually under adverse wind conditions. Many old-timers have adopted the modern shooting head in both floating and sinking versions backed with monofilament running line. Line weights 7 through 9 are most popular. A few casters use even heavier shooting heads, but in my opinion this is unnecessary and makes more work out of casting.

Any reasonably talented fly-rod man can also cover his fish with an 8-weight, forward-taper line. I use one that handles easily up to 30 yards under optimum conditions, and to 25 yards when the wind is blowing whitecaps on the lower pools of the Eel and Klamath. For morning and evening casting when there are no winds, I sometimes use a 7-weight, which picks up and shoots pleasantly to 75 or 80 feet. This all-white line is beautiful to use over dark water, because I can follow my drift with no difficulty. Shooting heads and lines of these sizes must be coupled with a fairly powerful 9- or 9½-foot rod for the most miles of uncomplicated casting.

You also need a sturdy fly reel, one that will hold 30 yards of fly line, and about 100 yards of 18-pound-test backing. For leaders on a floating line I use 9-footers tapered from .022 at the butt to .014 or .010 at the tippet. Chest-high waders with felt soles or chains are absolutely essential if you want to keep your shirttails dry.

Zane Grey used to fall in the Rogue fairly regularly when he was operating around Grants Pass. They still tell the story about how Grey lost his straw hat, full of flies, which was fished out of the river and sold by an enterprising gent in the local pub. In time, quite a few of these fly-draped hats were in circulation. But usually a sudden dunking in big water doesn't provide so much entertainment. I am of the felt-soled school on Pacific streams, but many riffle birds swear by the chains. In any case, avoid rubber-bottomed footwear.

In some years everything is right, and after a period of blue sky or even moderate rains the streams may clear enough to go out and take a steelhead for Christmas, using the fly. There is no season when the angler has a better chance at large, bright fish than in the winter. Winter-run trout are heavier, more numerous, and more commonly found in most coastal rivers. But dark, wet days hang like a curse when only deep-fishing with spoons and roe will find the steelhead.

Some streams, like the North Umpqua and Rogue in Oregon, which have good summer and autumn runs, stay clear and can be fished late in the season. Then there's the Nestucca, Siletz, Coquille, and Alsea, which get started in late autumn and offer good winter fly fishing. The Deschutes is still a fine summer and autumn river but no winter stream. Washington has the Skagit, Stillaguamish, Sky-komish, Cowlitz, and Green rivers at the head of the list for winter fly fishing, while California turns out giant trout in the lower pools of the Eel River. The Klamath and Smith get large winter runs, but these streams soup up in the rain. The Klamath left redwood logs on top of boulders, 30 feet over normal level, one winter. Of course, the migration in the Columbia River watershed extends up into the Snake and Salmon rivers of Idaho, but there is only a limited amount of summer and fall fishing there. The better part of the run appears in the northeastern Oregon streams. There are about seventy-five good winter steelhead rivers in the three coastal states, and again as many on the British Columbia mainland, Vancouver Island, and the Queen Charlottes.

As a fly-fishing game, the hunt for steelhead is in a class by itself. Mahah comes and Mahah goes, and you can run out of alarm clocks. But gents like Pop Morris will stand squarely among the riffle birds as long as the fish come back to their rivers.

Clinic

Steelhead hold in the same lies throughout the season. Even if a fish vacates a spot and moves on upstream, an-other steelhead will replace him. Of course, floods and drought may change the character of the water, but familiarity with a particular river is a great angling advantage. On strange rivers where the lies are unknown, the best approach is to cover the water in a series of drops by quartering your casts upstream when using a floating line, gradually lengthening each cast before wading to the next position. With a fast-sinking shooting head the casts can be made quartering downstream (as illustrated).

Polarized glasses are a big help in locating the dark forms of resting steelhead in summer water but in the high, usually off-color flow of winter the only option is to swim the fly as slowly and as deep as possible. Winter fish are most reluctant to leave the bottom. Unless the fly ticks against an occasional rock, it is swimming too high. Weighted flies, with wire-wrapped bodies, optic heads, or bead-chain eyes can make a critical difference by increasing the sink rate—and should be included in your box.

Quartering the casts

11

READING THE RINGS

I've never been fooled so completely as I was that first morning on Lake Taupo. The morning sun had just begun to show over a distant ridge across Western Bay when the trout started to rise. The fish worked from within a few yards of shore to far out in the lake, coming up in classic suction rises, making little whorls that spread out in great rings on the mirrorlike surface. We had been sleeping aboard Ron Houghton's launch, *Manunui,* and while he made the breakfast fire Dick Younger and I waded out on a gravelbar flailing our dry flies over one big rainbow after another. There were only a few spent naturals on the water —which should have tipped us off—but in our enthusiasm we began changing patterns, knowing that the next choice would be *it*. I must have put a dozen different floaters over countless trout without a sign of interest. Dick was having the same results.

Finally a trout came up about 10 feet in front of me. I saw the flash of silver before the fish even touched the surface. Its huge jaws opened and closed, expelling bubbles through its gills and making an audible sucking sound as it completed the lazy arcing rise. If a fat Green Drake had been sitting on the water it would have made sense, but seemingly that trout rose to nothing. The idea had already occurred to me that the fish were taking nymphs in the surface film, or perhaps feeding on almost microscopic midges; but the only sign of life, other than the trout, was a small, almost transparent minnow. Trout don't *rise* to baitfish, I reasoned; they run after them, slash at them, or chase them into the gravel. But I tied on a silver-bodied streamer and it no sooner hit the water than a 4-pound rainbow came straight from the bottom and inhaled it.

Of course, my "discovery" was no novelty to Ron Houghton, who has been guiding in New Zealand for twenty-eight years. Taupo's big trout feed on juvenile whitebait (actually no relation to a minnow, but a type of smelt), which shoal and swim rather feebly just under the surface. Whitebait are so vulnerable to these huge rainbows that the trout can pop them off in a practiced, leisurely style that would completely deceive the dry-fly man.

A rise is broadly defined as a surface disturbance made by a fish feeding upon insects. It usually looks like outward-spreading rings. However, the experienced angler can often see more than the beginner can in a rise, because its character frequently reveals what the fish is feeding on or, equally important, how it is feeding. Many years ago, G. E. M. Skues, in his classic book *The Way of a Trout with a Fly*, described numerous rise types: the leaping rise to airborne insects; the kidney-shaped double whorl to a large floating dun; the suction rise to medium-size floating flies; the sipping rise to the smallest floating duns, spinners, and midges; the slashing rise at running caddis and stoneflies; the head-and-tail rise to spent mayflies or their nymphs suspended in the surface film; the bulging rise to nymphs emerging from the bottom; the tailing rise for bottom food; and the false rise that materializes on the surface only after the trout has investigated and refused an artificial. Even the recognition of a refusal rise has some value. The ability to recognize all these different feeding postures on the part of a fish can save the angler many frustrating hours.

There are several factors that give specific characteristics to a rise: the size of the food object, its movement, and its position with relation to the surface. A large, active insect such as a dragonfly will trigger an eruptive, slashing rise, whereas a tiny, immobile midge floating on the surface may disappear in nothing more obvious than a dimple. However, some rises occur below the surface and create only a bulge in the water or are visible in a mere flash as sunlight reflects from the side of a turning trout.

First let's examine the sequence of events that form a typical mayfly hatch.

The transformation of the nymph to a winged adult begins when the nymph releases its grasp on the streambed and rises to the surface, drifting downstream with the current. It is capable of swallowing water, contracting its muscles, and exerting pressure on the cuticle region of the thorax, thereby freeing itself from its shuck. The skin starts to split while the nymph is several inches below the surface, and by the time the nymph reaches the top, the molt is usually complete. For the next thirty to sixty seconds the mayfly rides its cast-off nymphal skin downstream like a raft, shaking its wings to open the folds in which they were tightly compressed while still in the nymphal stage. Now as a dun or subimago the mayfly flies from the water and seeks a streamside shelter among vegetation where it will remain hidden overnight.

So in the typical mayfly hatch the trout position themselves first to capture the nymphs in their transit from the streambed to the surface. Stomachs of trout caught at this time will contain a large percentage of partly transformed insects. The fish usually lie just below the surface and take the rising nymphs in a rolling motion that causes a visible bulge in the water. Occasionally a dorsal fin or tail will show. As the mayfly emergence progresses and more nymphs survive to reach the surface, you may begin to see head-and-tail rises as the trout take the drifting duns that are now on top. Though the fish still display the same porpoising motion as in the bulge rise, they are now actively surface-feeding and it's time to switch from an artificial nymph to a dry fly. Toward the end of the hatch, when these subimagoes (which look softer and duller in color than the adult) are abundant, the rises will become splashier as more duns are airborne.

The final event (which in the angler's frame of reference is still a "hatch") is the mating flight. On the following morning, as the air warms, the mayfly undergoes a second molt, transforming from a subimago to an imago or spinner. Depending somewhat on weather conditions, it continues to rest in shelter until midafternoon. Then the males take wing and form the mating swarm, a loosely formed assemblage of up to hundreds of individuals, each alternately rising and falling through a space from a few inches above the water to about the highest level of streamside vegetation. After the swarm has formed, females start joining it individually. Almost at once, each is seized by a male, and mating takes place on the wing. The act may last from thirty seconds to three minutes. At its conclusion the female leaves the swarm to deposit her eggs, after which she almost immediately dies. The male rejoins the swarm and may mate again. In fact, if the weather is cool the male may survive for a second day and, as death approaches, fly away from the stream and die at some distance from water. Nevertheless, the surface will be littered with dead or spent spinners.

Initially, a mating flight creates extremely showy rises. The activity of the insects in their rapid hovering dance over the surface causes the trout to leap and slash at their ephemeral targets. The dry-fly angler may get a strike at the very instant the artificial touches the surface not only from below but often from fish that leap over the fly and take on the way down. As the flight subsides and the spent spinners lying inert in the surface film with wings out-spread become more and more numerous the trout settle down to a confident sipping as they gorge on the motion-less insects. The strike at an artificial now becomes no more than a pluck, which despite its innocence may hide a very large trout.

A stonefly emergence, and the types of rises it creates, is characteristically different. Unlike most mayflies, the stonefly nymph crawls out on the shore or the side of a rock when transforming into the winged adult. There is no helpless subimago drifting on the current. However, when stoneflies swarm on their mating flight the trout go absolutely berserk. The female stonefly may use one of two methods of egg laying: by the flying and dipping method, in which she touches the surface of the water with the posterior end of her abdomen while the eggs are released; or by releasing the eggs as she swims on the water, usually heading across and upstream. In the latter method, which is common to the larger species, the females create a considerable disturbance, leaving a wake behind them as they swim powerfully across the surface. It's not surprising that trout literally charge at a natural or an imitation. A slash rise is typical of the stonefly hatch. Interestingly, from the angler's point of view, the same drag that would be the bugbear of working an artificial over trout coming to a mayfly subimago is now something of an advantage. Cast across and downstream, an artfully worked imitation duplicates the activity of the egg-laying female.

When trout are rising steadily in slow water making dimples, chances are that the fish are feeding on midges. These tiny mosquitolike insects not only breed abundantly but are greatly relished by fish. Unlike most other aquatics, midges pass through several generations in the course of a single year. For this reason there are midges on the water every month of the season constantly developing through the various stages of their life cycle. Trout become very selective about feeding on midges at times, and even 2- or 3-pound fish will be found gorged with the larvae and pupae (which are taken more readily than the adult). When mature, the larvae measure less than ¼ to about ⅜ inch in length. They may be green, black, brown, or, most commonly, red. (The bloodworms or their dull-colored relatives burrow in the muck of river- and lakebeds and subsist largely on dead organic matter.) The pupal state occurs when the larvae rise to the surface; pupae hang vertically in the water, head up and tail down, with their gills in the surface film. Both the head and the tail of the pupa have distinctive hairy appendages, as well as an enlarged thorax and folded but visible wings. Trout often take the larvae at the surface and always come to the top for drifting pupae; thus feeding signs are evident even in the subaquatic stages.

It's the little dimples that occur as regularly as raindrops on the surface which reveal the midge rise. There are two important things to know: the imitation should be dressed on a #18 or #20, 2X long hook with just enough hackle to buoy it up on the surface film, which is where the trout are feeding; and the most effective way to work the midge imitation is usually in a dead drift after casting to the rise across and upstream. At times the effectiveness of the fly is increased if it's moved slightly with the rod as a rising fish is approaching.

In contrast to the midge-feeding trout, a fish feeding on caddisflies may appear as a "tailer" in shallow water with its head down and tail up grubbing along the bottom, or toward evening come to the surface in splashy rises. Caddisflies make up one of the four most important sources of food for fish because of their wide distribution, great numbers, and relative availability. Every kind of habitat has certain species of caddis adapted to it. Some spend their aquatic lives in stone cases glued to the surface of rocks or logs in the fastest waters; others, dragging bulky cases of sticks or leaves, crawl among the weeds of the quiet water of ponds or on the bottom of stream pools.

Fish consume them in all stages: as larvae picked off the rocks of the stream bottom and eaten case and all; as pupae in their cases transforming, or swimming or crawling up from the cocoons of pebbles or sticks to take wing as adults; and finally, during mating or egg-laying flights, when they are swarming over the rapids or dancing above a quiet pool in the evening. Some of the more important species (such as the white miller, autumn phantom, and black dancer) bring on heavy rises at times. Because of this insect's erratic mothlike flight, trout often jump clear of the water to catch one, and in general the angler who works his artificial in short pulls across the surface will earn more strikes.

The last important group of flies to the angler are the related damselflies and dragonflies. Both members of this group prefer quiet water for living. Favorite habitats are the margins of ponds and lakes, especially among the weeds. Although they are more common in lakes, a few damselfly nymphs almost certainly will be harbored in the trailing grass along the margin of a stream. Among the stones and waterlogged trash of the pools of many trout streams will be found the squat nymphs of the dragonfly. Carnivorous both as nymphs and adults, dragonflies prey on all types of small insects, crustaceans, and other living creatures of a size that they can capture. The nymphs of the larger dragonflies are even known to take small fish in their extensible lower lip, which is fitted with efficient hooks.

Despite the fact that damselflies usually hover out of the range of surface-feeding fish, they are comparatively feeble aerialists. They habitually rest on reeds and stumps along the water's edge, particularly when the sun is bright. Often those big, explosive rises made by bass or trout around emergent vegetation are aimed at careless damsel-flies as they seek a resting place. Dragonflies, on the other hand, are perhaps the fastest and most skillful fliers among the aquatics—they do attract some wild leaps from trout and bass.

Of course, there are no cut-and-dried answers to every situation. A cloud of flies over the water is sometimes ignored, sometimes taken greedily; and we are apt to find fish feeding in a variety of ways. However, the character of a rise can often provide the necessary clue to how each fish can be caught.

Clinic

No rise form is more exciting (or more productive of big fish) than the slashing attacks of trout feeding on giant stoneflies. There are a number of insects in the order Plecoptera, and the females of some species skim swiftly over the surface from the bank to fast water to drop their eggs, then rush back to land; other species take wing and fly out to a riffle and literally dive into the water when ovipositing, then pound the surface violently to get airborne again. In either case, fishing these emergences is an adventure far removed from conventional dry-fly practices.

The premier stonefly in Western waters, *Pteronarcys californica,* better known as the "salmon fly," begins hatching in April in California and continues until July in Montana. The salmon fly draws crowds of anglers to many famous rivers in an almost carnival atmosphere. The fiberglass and rubber traffic on Henrys Fork of the Snake, the Big Hole, and the Madison can be bumper to bumper. Float fishing is the ideal way to pursue a salmon fly hatch, as it is a movable feast with the action progressing a few miles upstream each day; stoneflies respond to the warming water and are most active at temperatures between 55°F and 60°F. Significant stonefly hatches (*Pteronarcys dorsata*) occur in Midwestern and Eastern states, on such rivers as the Pere Marquette in Michigan and the Big Delaware between New York and Pennsylvania; while these do not reach the proportions of Western emergences, they produce exceptional fishing in the month of June.

12

SUMMER TROUT

Summer trout cruising in clear water are extremely hard to catch. Although you may see them from the bank, to wade in and begin casting will usually send them running for cover. I watched three good browns cruising the Arkville flat of the Bushkill one afternoon, but each time I attempted to cast near them the flash of my line coming at the surface made them dart away. I walked back to the railroad station where Dan Todd worked and told him about the fish. He said that with any luck at all the trout would be feeding in the rushes along the bank at sundown and we could catch some by wading where they had been cruising. I would have been less awed if he had predicted

the collision of Halley's comet with the earth. There are habit patterns that you and I recognize—like a man's tendency to stand with his back to a fire—but it didn't occur to me that there was any logic in the habits of fish. Dan reasoned that the lush mayfly hatches were over now, and, since it was late in July, the trout would come looking for the fat reddish-brown caddisflies that hatched in the weeds at dusk.

We returned to the flat that evening; wading from hummock to hummock, then across the muddy bottom, we came to a firm shingle in midstream. Dan started by casting a small stiff-hackled dry fly in the rushes, back where I had been hiding earlier in the day. His fly landed in the reeds, and very gently he drew it into the mouth of a waiting trout. I had to change flies several times before I found one with a hackle stiff enough to guard the hook point from snagging, but then, copying Dan's technique, I caught two very respectable trout and lost a third. On the way home that night Dan said that someday I might make a fly fisherman, but first I had to observe stream life rather than just look at it.

Now, many years later, it is evident that trout pay the fiddler when the fiddling is done. Although Dan couldn't tell me the scientific name of an insect, he recognized the important ones found along his streams and studied their behavior. The fact that the great red sedge were running up and down the reed stems and depositing their eggs in the water was plain to Dan.

You will see plenty of caddisflies this summer, regardless of where you fish. In some states, such as Michigan, the best of the fishing is ahead in the month of August, when the big white caddis, or white miller, will appear on lower peninsula streams. The little fawnish-colored grannom, or shad fly, of the East may still be on the water in early July, but, for reasons best understood by trout, the shad fly doesn't always bring a heavy feeding period.

Adult caddisflies can be recognized by their wings, which are tentlike—not flat like a moth's, although there is a superficial resemblance between the two. In the air they have a crazy, erratic flight that will remind you of a horde of clothes moths that have just escaped from a closet. The larvae of the caddis live in those little stick, stone, and weed cases you've seen glued to rocks. Some species build portable ones so that the worm can pull his home along by extending the forepart of his body. When the larva has grown sufficiently, the open end of the case is blocked and the "worm" goes through a pupal stage, during which time the body and wings develop. Then the insect emerges, swims to the surface, sheds the pupal case, and becomes airborne; the wings are immediately effective. Dan always translated this in terms of nymph fishing as the signal to use caddis imitations that he worked in short jerky movements from the bottom to the surface.

Although caddisflies are found in all kinds of habitat, the kind of river in which they are most abundant is one with weed beds, where the gravel and sand show clearly in patches that shine or shade with the rippling of the surface. The upper Ausable in New York, Silver Creek in Idaho, and the Little Deschutes in Oregon are all good examples of this type. Downstream dry-fly fishing is as traditional in the West as upstream is in the East, and perhaps in the lush rivers spanning the Rockies there is good reason for it.

During the mating flights of the adult caddis, when they swarmed over the river, Dan was really at his best. He'd put on a heavily hackled sedge pattern, either a Great Red or a Silver Sedge, and cast downstream, then work the fly back very fast, skittering it over the water by raising his rod tip and stripping line at the same time. When trout really boiled to a caddis hatch, Dan never fished the natural float, mayfly-style. The method of retrieve gives a dimension to an artificial fly beyond its size, shape, and color.

Of the two groups of winged flies favored by trout, Dan believed the mayfly to be more easily imitated than the caddis. Most upright-winged dry flies represent various mayflies. With a color range from white to black and species numbering in the thousands, the traditional pastime of matching a single mayfly with feathers and silk easily explains why there are so many fly patterns. When alive and resting on the water, the wings of the natural are held upright. When dead, or "spent," mayflies sprawl on the surface with their wings in a horizontal position; these are imitated by spentwing-type dry flies.

The mayfly lives most of its life underwater as a nymph, during which time it goes through a series of molts until it reaches full size. When the time for casting off this nymphal shuck draws near, the wing pads become larger and darker in color, a point which fascinated Dan, as he felt that through familiarity with the nymph he could predict when a hatch would begin. This never worked in practice, however, even with the early-season mayflies, for whom the emergence period is very sharply defined. The nymph then swims to the surface, where the skin splits and the subimago, or dun, airs its opaque wings. The wings dry and expand in less than a minute and the sober gray dun flies to the shoreline foliage. It is a dangerous minute for the helpless mayfly, drifting high and easy on the whim of every current; just the way your Hendrickson, Quill Gordon, or Blue Dun floats back downstream. This is basic, and easy, imitation.

We had just one nocturnal mayfly hatch in our region that was worthy of attention, and that was the Green Drake. Two other hatches would come late in the afternoon, the March Brown and Quill Gordon. Just over the mountains to the north in the Schoharie watershed and also to the south in the Big Delaware watershed they would get a good Light Cahill hatch. I guess the Esopus was even more prolific in those days; every time we fished there during the mayfly season Dan would come home with a jar of specimens that he had never seen before.

In the summer months, however, the stonefly was much more important to the trout, especially in the very fast water below Phoenicia. When the mayfly was "off" the big fish just wouldn't budge except for large wet flies. It's interesting to compare this bouldery river with a sand- and gravel-bottomed stream like the Au Sable in Michigan, for instance, or the New Fork in Wyoming, where burrowing mayflies will still be hatching late in July. Hatches from boulder-strewn rivers become very sporadic as the summer progresses and the quality of the dry-fly fishing, in strictly mayfly style at least, tapers off.

Stoneflies are insects of fast water. Not only do they

inhabit the rapids, but the nymph moves so rapidly that anglers turning over rocks on the stream bottom seldom see them. It was Dan's contention that the effectiveness of big wet flies at night was due solely to the activity of stonefly nymphs. He claimed that he would see them scuttling along the bottom when he was eel-spearing with a carbide light. Admittedly the stonefly nymph is carnivorous, eating sprawler mayflies, midges, and other small animals found in fast water, so this noctural activity made sense to Dan. He fished two large wet flies in fast water on the evenings we went out, working them in rapid strokes like you'd retrieve a bucktail. The method is traditional to Eastern anglers and is practiced in some parts of the West. But in sombrero country anglers get consistently good daylight fishing with larval stonefly imitations because of the numerous swift, bouldery rivers that breed these insects in abundance; their late-spring or early-summer emergence causes a feeding spree among big trout comparable to the burrowing mayfly hatches of the East. Stonefly hatches are of comparatively minor importance on Eastern waters, although you'll find their nymphal shucks on the rocks of almost every freestone stream, and hors d'oeuvre–size portions in the stomachs of big browns and rainbows.

Bees and beetles are such desirable trout foods that Dan once said he could go through an entire season using a McGinty wet fly and a wet Leadwing Coachman. I don't think this narrow view would prove effective early in the season, but certainly after the month of July these airborne insects and their imitations find a welcome audience among the fish. The McGinty pattern, old as it may be, is still one of the best Western trout flies in the hot summer period. Ants and grasshoppers are two other easily imitated terrestrials that trout relish late in the summer. Flying ants usually begin appearing over Eastern waters about the third week in August, and because of their apparently high nutritive value, fish readily come to the surface for them. Except on the Big Delaware, we never had flying-ant swarms in the Catskill region to the extent that I saw them years later in Maine, when every brook trout in the Fish Chain of Lakes was on the rise. Grasshoppers, however, are seldom so abundant as they are on Western meadow-type streams. It's the rivers in the Rocky Mountains and down into the range's coastal drainage area that produce real 'hopper fishing late in the summer. The McMurray Ant pattern and a Letort Hopper (or a dry Muddler Minnow) are high on my list as August essentials.

Grasshopper patterns are usually most effective when fished close to the bank, where trout look for these insects. Don't be afraid to slap your fly down on the water so that it arrives like the real thing. Dan's favorite method of fishing a 'hopper imitation was to use a very long fine leader: casting downstream, he'd hit the surface within an inch of the bank. Then he'd twitch the fly a few feet upstream, let it drift back, and repeat the process. His leader was largely responsible for the fly's lifelike appearance, so pin this inside your hat. The butt consisted of 66 inches of .018; then he tied on a 6-inch strand of .010. These were all step-down diameters to a 20-inch tippet of .008. It's a wonderful leader for cautious trout and there's little or no surface disturbance because of its slightly over 9-foot length.

One of the periods that Dan never liked was in later summer, when the trout had a taste for midges. Actually, adult midges are on the water every month of the year, and midge larvae are constantly being eaten by fingerling trout. There are periods in the summer, however, when big trout get a craving for these tiny two-winged flies, and I have opened browns of 2 and 3 pounds in weight whose bellies were gorged with thousands of larvae and adults. Midge imitations consist either of a body with no wings or tail,

tied on a #18 or #20 hook, or simply a few turns of hackle
and just the faintest suggestion of a body. I doubt if the
trout see much more than pinpoints of light on the surface
when they look for midges.

Dan fished his imitations in or just below the surface
film, keeping all except the last few feet of his leader floating. The drift had to be perfectly natural, with no rod
movement and no drag from the line. It was just a case of
waiting for the pluck of a rolling trout. The awkward part
about this method is that one has to use very fine leader
points and fragile hooks. There was no such thing as nylon
then, and finding reliable silkworm gut drawn to 5X was
next to impossible. I abandoned the method one morning
below Forked Eddy when I rose fish after fish and broke off
every time.

With modern-day terminal tackle the percentage
would be in your favor, but the interesting part of Dan's
approach was that he finally ignored midge fishing as such
and used long-hackled wet spiders. These were tied very
carefully, usually in shades of gray, with the soft sparse
hackle about twice the length of the hook shank. Underwater the hackles pulled flat against the hook when he retrieved and rose slowly upward during the pause. These
old-fashioned spiders have a remarkably lifelike action, but
for no reason that Dan could fathom trout usually take
them especially well when midging. There are two other
seemingly unexplainable possibilities for good fishing during the midge periods—a small bucktail such as the brown-
and-white Dace pattern, and a spider-type dry fly.

Dragonflies, or so-called darning needles, are the
large, heavy-bodied, horizontal-winged insects that fly
swiftly over a summer pond. They are such skillful flies that
they seldom contribute much to the trout's diet. But the
big green darning needle deposits her eggs in the stems of
aquatic plants, as does the more slender and delicately

built damselfly. The damsel is immediately distinguished from the dragon in that its wings are held in a vertical position. It is in the nymphal stage that both these insects fall prey to trout, especially in weed-rimmed ponds and slow, grassy-banked rivers. During the period of abundance in later summer smallmouth bass will leap from the water trying to catch them, and oftentimes brown trout will go on a hot-weather damselfly orgy.

Dan Todd used a rather large Silver Docter wet fly to simulate the rapidly moving damsel. The adult natural is a brilliant metallic color, and any bright pattern with splashes of red, blue, and silver fished very rapidly on the surface will often work, even though the fly is slightly submerged. Brightly colored bucktails are also good, but at risk of being repetitious I must say that the Muddler Minnow should be your first choice. Fish it dry, and work it in swift strokes across the surface.

There are many other insects of summer importance, but no matter what appears over the water, all you have to remember is that this is the period when you have to change your methods of casting and retrieving quite frequently. Don't do all your casting upstream, and don't bring the fly back without trying to imitate the action of the natural insect. An artificial fly has only size, shape, and color. Try to give it that fourth dimension.

Clinic

Dan Todd was the stationmaster for the Ulster and Delaware railroad stop overlooking the East Branch at Margaretville, New York. Dan and the railroad are long gone, as is most of the river we fished (now under the Pepacton Reservoir), and, while his concepts of fly fishing may seem very basic—his was the wisdom of a half century ago—the message is clear: *Observe* stream life, don't just look at it. John Merwin pointed out to me that grasshopper imitations fish best late in the morning and early afternoon when these insects are most active streamside; and that switching to caddis or mayfly imitations when the sun is off the water is often more productive. In retrospect, I can recall a number of occasions when bank-feeding trout suddenly moved midstream and lost interest in my 'hopper patterns. Observations of this kind pay off.

Let there be no doubt, trout can become very selective at times. We see this most often on streams rich in insect life, such as the Henrys Fork of the Snake, the Bow River, or the Big Delaware, where several different species of mayflies or caddis can be hatching at the same time; you may find Pale Morning Duns (*Ephemerella invaria*), Light Cahills (*Stenacron canadense*), and Green Caddis (*Rhyacophila lobifera*) emerging simultaneously, only to find the trout prefer one to the others. (During a recent multiple hatch, I discovered the fish were feeding almost exclusively on flying ants, which I didn't even see on the water during the first hour of fishing. I had been distracted by the more visible mayflies.) At times, hatches and spinner falls will occur simultaneously, and trout may largely ignore the active duns to gorge on the easily captured spent insects—the perfect time for a spinner pattern.

covered monster from the sunken gardens of Okeechobee.
I have many recollections of fish running into dense mats
of foliage, where for a minute or two the monster's struggling tail stood upright out of the water, a sign of departure
and of an angler's poor judgment. No, the place for light
lure casting is clear water, or else a shallow lake where the
obstacles are no more formidable than an occasional tree
stump. But these waters are common everywhere; they are
the town creeks and village ponds where you and I do most
of our fishing. Here the baby baits are making a real score.

Whenever John Pope came to town he was like a cornered bear among a pack of dogs. Everybody wanted to
draw him out, to learn what manner of magic he used in
catching bass, for in the country where the Neversink joins
the Delaware he loomed great among anglers.

John was faithless to his own conspiracy, because he
finally confessed he whittled plugs no bigger than a peanut, and these tiny lures made of hard cedar were taking
the measure of every smallmouth for miles around. This
was before midget plugs were known, except among whit-
tlers of the Midwestern states, where light lures soon came
into vogue. But few people had the patience to emulate his
work, and even fewer understood the mechanics of tackle
well enough to throw the plugs John gave them. I met John
Pope when I was quite young, and I'll never forget the first
time he allowed me to go fishing with him. It was a hot
summer day.

Nobody bothered about the backwaters along the
Delaware, but John vanished from the main stream shortly
after we turned the bend at Forked Eddy. He was obviously
on the other side of the woods, so I set out to find him.
After pushing through a jungle of sumac I reached a place
where the backwater flattened into a broad pool. There
was John kneeling on the bank behind a deadfall getting
ready to cast. Even from where I stood there were easily a

dozen bass visible, drifting slowly across the middle of the pool. John flipped his plug well beyond them, and it came down with a faint *splat* after checking his cast high in the air. He held the rod high over his head, and the line didn't touch the water anywhere near the bass. After the lure sat there for a moment, he jiggled it two or three times and began a slow retrieve that would intercept the small-mouths.

The instant the plug appeared near the school, several of them milled around as though they might take it; John stopped swimming the plug, but the fish lost interest. He rose carefully to his feet and began retrieving once again, an easy paddle, paddle, stop. Two smallmouths rushed to the bait, and John jerked it clean off the water. The bass were startled. I was amazed.

"Too small," said John. "Next time I'll get that big one; darn fool is always looking the wrong way."

I don't know if John ever caught that big one, but his attitude sums up the professional approach to midget plugging. This is not a loud method of fishing. Use a bigger plug when you want to attract any and all fish from un-known distances. Midget plugs have a great deal in com-mon with bass bugs in that they are most effective when used over an individual fish—one that you find feeding— or used in a lair where you know a bass should be.

I think the most sparkling tribute paid to the modern midget plug is the number of brown trout that are being caught by bass fishermen in waters where both species are found. For sheer skulduggery, the brownie makes the smallmouth look like a bumpkin. Our bass has a native wisdom, but occasionally he raises like a wakened lion to roar his displeasure in the face of a lure that would send a trout into fits of laughter. Of course even a brown trout will blow his cork once in a while, but until the midget casters got to work we seldom heard reports such as those made in recent years—which claimed browns up to 17 pounds and more in weight.

I believe the strike of a bass to the midget plug is a convincing demonstration of the difference between baby baits and the standard plugs. The strike is usually nothing more than a pluck or tug at the line, obviously made by a fish who is convinced that this is something to eat. Several times I have had bass play with the lure before attempting to swallow it, and invariably the plug is taken with an easy, confident turn—the strike of a fish who has been completely fooled.

For midget plugs, the baitcaster will want to use a 6- or 6½-foot rod. It cannot be too soft or bend too much in the butt or the lure won't go very far or very accurately. There are many small free-spool and level-wind reels to fit such a rod, and when filled with 6- or 8-pound-test monofilament line your equipment is complete. Of course the threadline angler can use his standard 6½- or 7-foot spinning rod and a lightweight reel with 4-pound-test monofilament. In either case, baitcasting rod or threadline, the angler makes no compromise with his method—the plug will respond as pointedly as a compass needle to the North Pole. I do think that a leader is important, however, if the angler is using braided line. (Although the new generation of anglers has been heavily influenced by monofilament, there are still many who prefer braided lines on revolving spool reels.) For baitcasting I would suggest a nylon leader about 5 feet in length so that the knot doesn't go down into the level-winding device. The leader is as much a shock absorber as it is a camouflage. As a rule the leader should have a barrel-and-snap swivel to attach the plug to, but you'll find that some surface plugs work much better without the swivel.

There are now dozens of good poppers, darters, jointed runners, injured minnows, and deep divers availa-

ble in the midget plug group. In actual weight they range
from less than 60 to 140 grains—several of them are
heavier than the specified ¼ ounce. One feature which
they all have in common is that they fall easily on the water,
making a wet *splat* instead of the wave-rocking plunge of
a heavier bait. There's no doubt that this sound can be
attractive to fish at times, as bass will frequently hit a motionless bait immediately upon landing.

Among the early additions to the midget plug family
was a peanut-size deep runner with a feather tail and a
propeller on its nose. This bait fished slow and deep and
ran up a good score on walleyes and bass along the Susquehanna, Delaware, and Shenandoah rivers. One plug I
came to depend on was one of the new darter-type baits in
a silver-flash finish; it has a slow, sweeping wobble and, for
noonday casting in shallow waters, the darter is particularly useful.

A baby torpedo plug accounted for several fine bass
one evening when it was jumped over the surface. The late
Jim Deren and I were fishing Cedar River Flow in the
Adirondacks and the day had been particularly dull. Jim
made one cast slightly beyond a brush sweeper and, to get

the bait clear, he pulled it off the water, hurdling the branches. Being in a puckish frame of mind, he continued to jump the plug back when a bass appeared from nowhere and caught the leaping minnow. We didn't need any further encouragement. Jim took two more smallmouths and I caught one using that skipping retrieve. But the bass were big ones for Cedar River, and we couldn't take them any other way. I have since made some very nice catches with the torpedo-type plug fished in the same manner when bass were at the surface chasing schools of baitfish.

Midget plugging is especially effective in clear water and during the late summer season when large bass are not active. I remember one bright day near Grindstone Island on the Saint Lawrence River, when a small deep-running plug took fish after fish in an area that had been thoroughly covered with standard-sized plugs. Hank Nelson had located a bay around one of the smaller islands where a great school of smallmouths gathered in hot weather. The bay was paved with small round stones laid close together and beaten down firmly by the waves. At the head of the bay a spring trickled in over a ledge of granite, and in the shadow of that cliff the bass lay undisturbed. One careless movement would scatter them.

There was no wind that day, and with our boat stationary in the cove we cast to the shoreline for almost an hour without getting a strike. I finally snapped on a tiny, jointed deep runner for no other reason except that this was the only plug we hadn't tried. In a matter of minutes the first smallmouth moved out of the shadows, following the plug almost to the boat before he swallowed it. The fish made a noble jump and my rod vibrated when he plunged under a flat rock to saw the line off, but his climactic action was dull by comparison with the sight of bass after bass coming out of the shadows to take the lure with each new cast. There are days like that. I landed five bass before giving the lure to Hank. While he was catching fish I worked a standard ⅝-ounce plug in the same places and caught absolutely nothing. Ever since we made this score, I have used nothing but midget plugs on that river, and, while I've probably passed up a few big muskie and pike because of it, my bass fishing has improved 100 percent. Only one muskie took the midget, and he submerged with the deliberate ease of a hippopotamus, holding the little yellow darter in his jaws. My line just wasn't strong enough.

Late-summer lake fishing is more difficult. In the early morning and late evening, surface midgets and darters will sometimes make a good showing. But if the weather is real hot and the bass are deep you'll need a plug that sinks way, way down, and here I question whether the baby plug has any more on the ball than a standard size. Most of us just don't catch the summertime bass because we're not fishing at the right depth. Often as not I find that a really heavy plug worked about 40 feet down is more effective than smaller baits which just don't have enough beef to sink that far. My enthusiasm for midget plugs stops about 5 feet below the surface, and unless I am river fishing where there are only occasional deep holes, a ¼-ounce plug is not my choice for a bottom-running lure. But the best we can hope for in any bait is that it overcomes a greater margin of angling error and provokes fewer interludes of silent contact with unseen fish. The technique is like bass bugging, and to my way of thinking the midget plug has all of the bug's virtues and none of its faults. Mouse, frog, or minnow, a ¼-ounce imitation doesn't give the bass much to ponder over—and that is as it should be.

Clinic

There is an infinite variety of midget plugs available today ranging from $\frac{1}{16}$ to $\frac{1}{4}$ ounce. Individually, they differ in size, shape, color, action or vibration pattern, and operable depth. All plugs regardless of weight can be divided into four categories: (1) surface plugs that float throughout the retrieve; (2) floating-and-diving plugs that can be worked slowly on the surface, then pulled underwater by speeding up the retrieve; (3) swimming plugs that slowly sink and have a vibrating or wobbling action when retrieved, such as the "countdowns"; and (4) deep diving plugs or "crank-baits," which are swimming lures with a big lip that causes the lure to plane deep. Plug selection depends on the type of cover or structure being fished. A shallow lily-padded

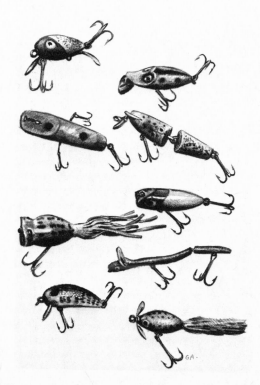

cove or a gravel point are ideal spots for a top-water plug at dawn and dusk, while a steep bank or channel edge footed by boulders or downed timber is the perfect situation for a crankbait during midday hours. In our Southern bass waters, particularly in Florida and Georgia, midget plugs and the essential light tackle are not as effective as they are in Northern lakes and rivers. However, I find midgets very effective in south Florida canals during clear water periods.

14

THE FINE ART OF THINKING BIG

Any Eastern fly fisherman making his first trip west is apt to think that Rocky Mountain fly tiers are really a bit over the hill. After he's dealt with double-domed trout on rivers like the Beaverkill and Ausable, a display of the local patterns in Livingston or West Yellowstone might shake the visitor down to his felt soles. Some of the flies in fashion are the size of a hummingbird and have no more character than a hank of hair wrapped on a hook. However, practical members of the sombrero set learned long ago that big trout won't usually rise to a bit of fluff, and to coax one to the surface requires a monumental reward. True, the micros developed for more gentle rivers have their place here also, but in the West extremes pay off.

Several years ago we floated a pair of double-enders down the New Fork to a long stretch where the river runs deep and foamy under a cut willow bank. Bill Isaacs and Larry Madison stopped at the first gravelbar and I rowed another half mile to the next pullout with Elmer George. It was early in the morning but there was already a nice hatch of small blue-colored mayflies on the river. They looked fairly close to a #14 Dark Hendrickson, so we went to work on the nearest risers that were popping away in midstream. We fished for about three hours, then took a coffee break.

Elmer said he'd released about 20 trout but his biggest fish wasn't much over 10 inches and most of them were 8- or 9-inch rainbows. I had the same results. This isn't *bad* fishing, but the New Fork holds much heftier trout. Hoping to find a better match with the natural, I had tried a Quill Gordon, a Blue Upright, and a Blue Quill, and Elmer had gone through the same routine.

There was a time when I'd have accepted the fact that the big ones just weren't feeding, but Western trout have their quirks. I tied on a #6 Goofus Bug, which looked about ten times larger than the ephemeral insect dancing in the air, and waded back into the stream. After covering a short distance along the willow sweepers, the surface exploded and I was fast to our first good fish of the day— a brownie of better than 2 pounds. By noon we had released a dozen trout in the 16- to 18-inch class.

When Larry and Bill came downriver to join us for lunch, they reported a similar experience. Mr. Madison is not only an exceptional fly tier but a keen observer of Western waters. We all agreed that while "matching the hatch" is a basic tenet of fly fishing, and without question a sound piece of advice, it is often true that it takes a veritable puffball—wholly unlike anything flitting in the air —to catch trophy trout in sagebrush country. The reason is probably nothing more profound than that big fish normally hold closer to the bottom than small trout, and, in heavy water, only a substantial food item would make swimming to the surface worth the effort.

During the early July salmon fly hatch, large fish do stay near the top to nail those fat stoneflies as they zoom over the water depositing their eggs. Almost instantaneous strikes are common then; the fly seldom floats more than a few feet if it's going to be taken at all. But the exception doesn't prove the rule.

I kept a careful set of notes that season on the hatches that occurred and my results with respect to what was happening at the time, and I collected hundreds of aquatic insects for later identification. It still makes interesting reading, but I have to admit the great majority of large trout (which I count from 18 inches or better than 2 pounds) fell to the dry Muddler, Goofus Bug, Irresistible, Grayback, and Joe's Hopper. None of these flies resembled the significant emergences that may have been in progress. I missed the salmon fly hatch by a week.

My fishing that summer was confined to the New Fork and Green in Wyoming, and the Madison, Big Hole, Missouri, and Beaverhead in Montana with a couple of visits to Georgetown Lake. I fished 89 days in all, for a total of 1,233 releases, with the largest trout a brown of 7 pounds, 5 ounces. There were several blank days, to be sure, but we also experienced 60- and 70-fish days on some of the floats. I know that if I had included streams of a different character, like Montana's Spring Creek or the spring creek feeding the Snake in Wyoming, it would have been a different picture entirely with #16 and #18 Light Cahill, Adams, Mosquito, and other miniskirted patterns taking the honors.

Unquestionably, getting a good high float in fast water is of prime importance in raising big trout. This also applies to low-silhouette patterns such as Bird's stonefly, Muddler, Joe's Hopper, and Sofa Pillow. It's when the fly is skimming along the top in a lifelike fashion that trophy fish respond. If it hangs back suspended in the surface film, the ratio of strikes goes down rapidly. To avoid this requires prime materials in the fly and a reliable flotant as well as a long leader and short, accurate casts. Even a scraggly deerhair fly should be tied with the finest gamecock hackles. Light-wire hooks are also an advantage on patterns with hackles ranging up to 1¼ inches in diameter. Many anglers feel that wings are not important on large dry flies, but they're a great help for visibility to the caster working in rough currents or poor light. Although deerhair is little used in the East it is virtually a *must* in the West.

Deerhair flies had their genesis in Oregon. Undoubtedly frustrated by trying to float a dry pattern on the tumbling waters of the McKenzie, Rogue, or Willamette, some unknown fly tier resorted to hollow-celled mule deerhair. When used in a wing the hair causes the fly to pop up to the surface after being sucked under. The first of these patterns was the Bucktail Caddis, a palmer-tied fly with its wings sloped back along the body. The Light Buck Caddis and the Dark Buck Caddis have been around since Hector was a pup.

Then someone discovered that the wings could be tied down both fore and aft and this evolved into a whole series of dry flies epitomized by the Horner Deer Hair and later the Goofus Bug on which the body and tail are formed by pulling deerhair back over the hook shank and securing it at the bend. The same idea was applied to nymphs such as the Henrys Lake pattern and the Shellback, but, of course, these have to be weighted.

I have caught trout on large dry flies when there

wasn't a sign of an aerial hatch, and, in examining their stomach contents, found the fish literally stuffed with bottom organisms such as snails, nymphs, and sculpins. Apparently they just couldn't resist a big floater.

One day on many-fingered Georgetown Lake in western Montana the red-sided rainbows gave us a fit on our deeply sunk shrimp imitations. The trout were in the shallow portions of the broad weed beds and for several hours the fishing was hot. Then it stopped. There were no surface rises until I saw a dragonfly dart over the water and perch on some emerged vegetation. A trout swirled nearby, evidently frustrated by its disappearance. I tied on a fluffy #6 Muddler and dropped it next to the weed patch and had an immediate strike. The fish took out my entire fly line and was into the backing before he rolled on the surface and displayed about 24 inches of crimson stripe— and was off. Disappointing perhaps, but the one opportunity to take a trophy trout came on an outsize dry fly.

Deerhair patterns are not the only type of fly that will bring big trout to the top. Variants, such as the light and dark patterns originated by Roy Donnelly (which are tied with mixed-color hackles two sizes larger than regular for any given hook number), work extremely well at times. Because of its air resistance due to the large diameter of the extended hackles it is almost impossible to bring a Variant down heavily on the surface of the water. It is a great boon to the mediocre caster and ideal for difficult trout. The fly does not imitate any particular insect, although it may suggest one, but it does have some of the ethereal qualities of many aquatics because it is delicate and rides high on the water.

The key in its design is the lightness of the hook. A light wire hook permits the use of minimum hackle, and when that hackle is long the hook will stand away from the surface, provided it is supported by an equally long tail. Furthermore, it falls easily on the water and has less tendency to drag on complex currents; it literally bounces over them. This ability to move almost independently is no small part of its attraction.

The Variant is most effective on swift water that is glassy or reasonably flat. In very turbulent runs the bulkier clipped-hair-bodied flies float better, and their larger impression against the surface is undoubtedly more useful in tempting trout to the top. However, on many rivers the problem fish are in the moderately swift places where artificials are easily distinguished from the real thing. There is a great deal of this type of water on the Firehole for example, and also on the Henrys Fork of the Snake. The stiff, long, sparsely dressed Variant is a brilliant suggestion of insect life under these conditions.

It is usually difficult for the amateur fly tier to find the quality spade and saddle hackles that are necessary in dressing a Variant; a rooster doesn't grow more than a half-dozen of the former, and commercial skinners are inclined to trim off the saddle hackles. For this reason, many of the popular patterns consist of two different mixed spades, such as ginger and grizzly or mahogany and grizzly. To get maximum flotation, do not make a body on the fly, but wind the hackles around two-thirds of the shank length of the hook.

Some years ago, and just before his passing, I fished with a fine gentleman and author, Claude Kreider. Among other things, he was a skilled rod builder, and with his home-glued sticks Claude laid out a beautiful dry fly.

It was my first visit to the Firehole in Yellowstone Park, and the river was alive with feeding trout that day. There was a hatch of black mayflies in progress, and the fish were greatly in evidence. A dozen widening rings in front of us caused me to joint my rod with trembling fingers. Under the sod bank right at our feet a handsome brownie rolled up to suck in a dun. We had found the Firehole at its best and there was nobody else on the river for at least a mile. I pawed hurriedly through my fly box and found a #12 Black Quill with just the right shade of hackle to match the natural.

Then I noticed Claude tying on a huge cream-colored Variant. I knew he usually wore glasses but my naïve observation about what was in the air and being accepted fell on deaf ears. Claude gave the Variant a good oiling, then tossed it out with wiggly S-casts and proceeded to catch trout. I did too. The difference was that he took a 4-pound rainbow and a brown of about 2½ pounds while I raised Merry Ned with yearlings. It wasn't long before I was borrowing his Variants.

There was no magic in his performance. Claude had fished the Firehole many times and, after slaughtering the innocents over a period of time, he had begun to experiment. He started by fishing a given hatch with flies that seemed to match the naturals, keeping note of his successes. Then he tried various outsize floaters on the same water. Even during a hatch of small ephemerids, trout—especially big trout—came for the large fly. Convinced by

repeated experiments, he began to fish large flies exclusively. The big fly has proved particularly valuable on swift
Western rivers because it floats high even on deep swirls
and riffled stretches of water. On such broken water, with
the trout's vision more or less obscured, any exact imitation of a natural hatch is of secondary importance. The
trick is to keep a "lively" fly dancing on its hackle points.

The big-fly story is, of course, contrary to accepted
dry-fly principles. It might also be added that *how* the fly
is fished is often diametrically opposed to standard technique. On rivers that run at a full gallop I cast the big dry
across and downstream about 90 percent of the time.
There are several reasons for this: It's too much work
banging away up the current in a really large river only to
get brief floats; the fly will behave in a more lifelike manner
on a rough surface when you can keep slack out of a line
and adjust its movement with your rod tip; and, contrary
to what one would expect and what one actually observes,
a big stonefly can swim like hell against a swift flow. Nature
designed the stonefly for highly oxygenated tumbling
riffles, and its skill as a sprinter is classic. In most cases I
imagine the trout mistakes the big artificial for a stonefly,
but whether this is so or not is less important than the
prevalent belief that a floater looks more lifelike when
riding completely free. This is a very fine point but it makes
a critical difference on boulder-studded Western streams.

Learning to cast a slack line is very easy. Correctly
executed, the slack-line cast is aimed directly down to the
position of the fish, but it should float about half that
distance. In other words, if the trout is holding 40 feet
away, you should drop the fly about 20 feet downstream
and cover the difference by shaking more line out.

There are several ways of making slack-line deliveries.
It's easiest for most people to false-cast in the usual man-

ner and, on the final stroke forward, stop the rod at a
45-degree angle; when the line begins to shoot, simply
wiggle the tip from side to side. This lateral motion will
create little curves in the outgoing line. Play with this for
a few minutes, and you'll find that you can make narrow or
wide elbows of slack with no effort. For most purposes,
seven or eight small curves should be enough.

When you drift the fly down on a fish, don't get the
slack concentrated in one big belly. It will get caught
broadside in the current and cause drag. As a tactical advantage, the initial presentation should be made in a perfectly natural float. After the cast is fished out, you can
begin animating the fly against a dragging line. So the rod
wiggling must be timed to distribute the curves through
the length of the cast.

There is only a shade of difference between a natural
and unnatural movement imparted to the fly in its drift
downstream. On individual rising fish an effort should be
made to get a drag-free drift on the first cast. The fly will
reach a point in its float when the trout either accepts or
rejects it, and, presuming the latter case, you must now
draw the floater back for a new cast. When working directly
down on a fish, this invariably requires pulling it over the
fish—a motion which is either going to excite a strike or put
the trout down. You will rarely get a second chance as you
might in upstream casting when the fly dances away on
tippy-toes. This is the moment when a fine-line point, a
long leader (preferably 12 feet), and a correctly hackled fly
make a critical difference. On slick water in particular,
coarse terminal gear is going to create a wake and spoil the
whole illusion.

Raise the rod slowly and begin twitching gently, bringing the fly upstream in short, pulsing strokes. If the fly is
standing up on its hackles and the fish doesn't respond

after it has moved a few feet, lower your rod and let the fly drift near it again. A keen fish sense helps at moments like this, but gradually you will learn to gauge the fly's action according to the response of the trout. Occasionally you might try skimming the fly away at a steady speed. As last-cast reeling has repeatedly proven, a positive and continuous flight often triggers blasting strikes. Although mayfly lore more or less conditions our thinking in terms of delicate ephemeral flutter, the fact is that many other insects, such as grasshoppers, dragonflies, and moths, disturb the surface greatly.

At dusk on July 21 in the year 1916, below Rabbit Rapids on the Nipigon River, Dr. W. J. Cook of Fort William, Ontario, hooked a fish, which after a few heavy surges ran into quiet water and pounded nose-down at the bottom. The play didn't last long, and, despite the fish's size as his guide heaved it in the boat, the doctor counted it as just another lake trout which they would save for breakfast. In the light of the lantern back at his tent the guide let out a whoop that brought the accident-conscious Cook on the run. It was a 14½-pound brook trout which was about to go under the knife. This rather casually taken trophy has stood as the world's record for sixty-nine years. Of all historical catches it seems to be one of the most difficult to top, as very few squaretails caught since have even come close to the Nipigon mark.

Today, except in the remote river systems of Argentina and Labrador, brook trout of over 5 pounds are comparatively rare, and, while we don't think of them especially as surface feeders, fully 30 percent of the fly-caught *Field & Stream* entries during the 1960s fell to large dry patterns. Streamer flies are more or less traditional fodder for squaretails, yet some of the best brook trout fishing I've enjoyed in Manitoba, Quebec, Ontario, and Maine has been during the early-summer mayfly hatches with fat 4-

and 5-pounders going for a huge floating Muddler twitched slowly over the surface.

I am a firm believer in matching the hatch. I've failed to take rising fish too many times to think otherwise. However, those nondescript puffballs that clutter the display cases of Western tackle shops represent a lot of common-sense fishing. In the last American stronghold of trophy trout it pays to think big.

Clinic

At first glance it might seem impossible, but there are several easy ways of getting a drag-free drift when fishing dry flies—or wets and nymphs—downstream, and one of the easiest to master is the lazy-S cast mentioned in this chapter. After making the forward cast and while the air-borne line is extending forward, simply waggle the rod from side to side as the line is shooting out. The line will fall to the water in a series of S curves, reducing drag on the fly itself until the current straightens the line. The size and number of curves in the line can be controlled by the size and force of your waggles in casting. With enough practice, you'll be able to put S curves in the leader end of the line, in the middle, only near the rod, or over the entire length of extended line as appropriate. As with the para-chute cast (as described in chapter 18), it's important to lower your rod tip to the water at the conclusion of the cast to be able to respond quickly in the event of a take. On very long casts, I prefer the parachute style of rod checking, as rod waggling creates friction on the line and reduces distance.

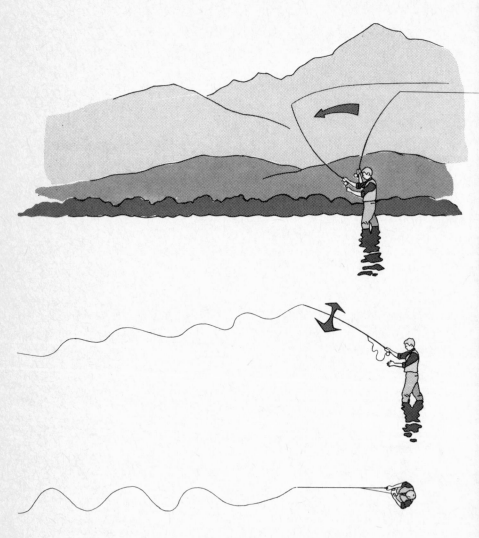

Wiggle cast

15

NYMPH IS NOT A DIRTY WORD

When you live on a river, as I have lived for most of my life, you soon come to realize how inconsequential your fishing skills are compared to the survival skills of a wild trout.

There was an undercut bank on the Beaverkill, near our cabin, that I was certain held an elderly brown with jaws like a nutcracker. For weeks I never even saw my fish, though I was on the water at all hours from late spring into autumn. A deeper, greenish pool above was calendar-cover beautiful and full of cooperative trout, but after the stream made its bend, and the current purled back under the hemlock roots and then spun away before dancing merrily over a pebbled riffle—that was the spot. I could smell it as sure as a coming rain in a dry summer. But the undercut was densely canopied by low-hanging boughs almost to water level, and the only way I could get a fly near those roots was by crawling on hands and knees and making a 30-foot cross-stream cast—usually with one elbow in the water.

It was a ridiculous performance, according to wife Patti, daughter Susan, Arnold Gingrich, Bedell Smith, Bert Lahr, and other critics who happened along. At one point I did consider cutting the boughs down, but that would be

unfair to my special tenant. Four times out of ten I'd throw my backcast into a hemlock behind me and pop my leader. Three times out of ten I'd manage to get my fly caught in the opposite boughs on my forward cast. And when a cast did arrive on the water, only one or two ubiquitous flame-bellied brook trout, so abundant in these upper pools, would appear, making me even more aware of a greater presence.

In my daily elbow exercise I tried every kind of fly in the box. Not even a Muddler caused a stirring in the under-cut. Toward the end of that season, when the water was quite low, I reverted to my Catskill boyhood and used a method one step above a wiggly garden worm. I attacked the problem from upstream with a small weighted nymph on a long, fine leader. I made a short cast and paid line out in the current, maneuvering the fly so that it drifted down into the hole to swim near the roots. Then I waited. Long minutes passed before I felt the tug, but instead of immediately boring back into his den, the trout came out, a sooty-black monster, probably momentarily blinded by sunlight. I splashed downstream, hoping to lead my prize away from the undercut. The fish helped by making one strong run, which left him belly-flopping in the riffle below—but this maneuver also snapped my tippet.

I have caught many trout greater in pounds than this one was in inches, and would have released it in any event. The point of my story is that even the most sophisticated trout—and a brown of about 18 inches on the upper Bea-verkill rates summa cum laude—can be taken on a nymph sooner or later. The versatility of this type of fly is remark-able.

There was another place downstream, a short deep run where the river spilled over barren bedrock in a foam-ing cascade; this was reliable for two or maybe three acro-batic 8-inch rainbows in the side pocket. But in that rushing water I was convinced no greater presence existed at all, unless it was ethereal (for some reason there was always an eerie golden light falling on that pool in the evening as though polarized through a stained-glass window). Nevertheless, it was a pretty spot in which to cast a fly while watching chipmunks scamper among the ferns. It was included in my daily schedule, which was less precise but as dedicated as any Swiss railroad's. (I can get sidetracked by a patch of wild strawberries.)

I must have fished the miniature cascade ninety times that season, from all angles with all kinds of flies. Even my rainbow friends were becoming reluctant, so I tried skimming a little gray caddis pupa over the surface to stir some interest. A darkly spotted brown came barreling out of the depths, and, after a long seesawing contest of surging runs against my 6X tippet, he was measured against my rod butt —19½ inches. The nymph had been taken when fished like a dry fly.

Fishing with an artificial nymph is the basic method of trout angling. The nymph will catch fish 365 days of the year—not always the largest and not always the most, but it will take them consistently. Equally important is the *method* of nymphing, because it teaches beginners everything they must know about trout habits and habitat. Nymph fishing can be successful in the coldest or hottest weather, in dead calm water or a raging torrent, and from the surface to the very bottom of those secret places where great trout hide.

Nymph fishing is old and its development has quite a history, but it did not become popular in America until about 1930. In the half century since, the totemization of G. E. M. Skues' *Minor Tactics of the Chalk Stream* has certainly inspired those who fish and those who write about it.

For any angling writer, it is a rare privilege not only to describe his country and time but to give perspective to the sport. Skues succeeded in doing this, but in a strangely delayed way.

It is hard to believe now, but once upon a time *nymph* was a dirty word. In the formal establishment of 1910, Skues was considered a heretic "dabbler in unworthy excesses" by many of his peers. Gentlemen belonged to the Houghton Club, marinated their Stilton in 150-year-old port, and fished with floating patterns. It has never been clear to me why a fly that is sunken, presumably the inferior condition in which artificials originated in the first place, should become the villain in a morality play. Yet within my own lifetime I recall nearly being drummed out of the corps for casting a nymph on the hallowed waters of the Risle. This French chalkstream was still immune to Skues' development by July of 1948, though God knows it is only a stone's throw across the Channel from Hampshire to Normandy. Yet the good word had not been passed.

I had caught and released three lovely trout that were obviously bulging in a slick run below the cider mill when our host, Edouard Vernes (who was flailing a dry fly upstream from me and catching nothing), came pounding down the bank and asked what manner of "bait" I was throwing into his river. He held my leader tippet between his fingers with a look of complete disdain and gurgled *nam-pff!* I thought he was going to have a stroke. If it hadn't been for an instant character reference from Charlie Ritz, who promised I would mend my ways, Vernes, a millionaire bank chairman who brooked no evil, probably would have snapped my 8½-foot CCF over his knee and sent me by square-wheeled tumbrel to the Bastille. The fact that I was demonstrating for Charlie how to fish a nymph was not mentioned until some years later in Ritz's book *A Fly Fisher's Life.* Even to think of teaching Charlie Ritz anything about trout was almost ludicrous, but my mentor himself had been insulated by the ground rules of chalkstream society. Eventually Charlie met Frank Sawyer, the doyen of nymph artists, and became a fanatic on nymphing. I have never met Frank Sawyer, but I was flooded with letters from Charlie describing how Sawyer did this or Sawyer did that. It was as though he had translated the Dead Sea Scrolls.

I learned the fundamentals of nymphing back in the 1930s. The only popular American patterns, then purveyed by William Mills and Son, were the flat-bodied, lacquered creations of Edward Ringwood Hewitt—a design also claimed by John Alden Knight, although I can't imagine why. These nymphs came like licorice sticks in three color combinations: black with a gray belly, black with an orange belly, and black with a yellow belly. I seldom caught many trout with these, so, like everybody else who took fishing seriously, I tied my own.

Some idea of where the nymph existed by 1936 can be found in a little 55-page book, *Tying American Trout Lures,* by Reuben R. Cross. Rube, the sage of Shin Creek, was a master craftsman, yet all he had to say about nymphs covered 4½ pages and concerned four patterns: the Guinea nymph, the Black-and-White nymph (grub), the Olive Wood-Duck nymph, and the Carrot-and-Black nymph. Dan Todd, Ray Neidig, Mike Lorenz, and quite a few other tiers in the Delaware Valley were experimenting with patterns.

Dan Todd was the Ulster & Delaware stationmaster in Margaretville. He amassed a considerable collection of trout foods perserved in formalin that he kept in his office. One morning a man named Olson (whom Dan detested for his murderous consistency in killing large quantities of trout with spoons and worms) saw a mason jar of pebble-type caddis cases sitting on his desk.

"What's them things?" Olson asked Todd.

Dan looked pained. "I just had an operation. Them's my kidney stones."

Olson stared closely at the jar. "God almighty! No wonder you can't fish!"

I was fishing mostly on the East Branch of the Delaware in those days, places like Fuller's Flat and Keener's Flat, which by any standard were classic runs. A Catskill flat was often several miles long, containing more riffles and rapids than still water.

It was April of 1936 when I caught my first big trout. The weather was cold and snowy and the river was running high. I was fishing a home-tied nymph by casting upstream and letting it sink close to my bank--which was no trick with a waterlogged silk line. I caught quite a number of trout that morning before getting stuck in the bottom, and when that brown finally came thumping to life it was the biggest thrill a fourteen-year-old boy could have. The trout was too big for my landing net, and I remember, after getting its head stuck in the mesh, wrestling my prize into a snowbank. I walked home, feeling like one big goose pimple, by way of the lumberyard, the butcher shop, the drugstore, and the ill-named Palace Hotel, making sure everybody in town saw my fish. Dan Todd weighed it at the railroad station—7 pounds, 2 ounces, not an adult trophy for the East Branch in those days, since fresh mounts in double figures to 15 pounds or more hung glassy-eyed on every saloon wall.

When I dressed the trout, some of the nymphs that filled its belly were still alive; its digestion rate had slowed almost to a halt in the near-freezing water. What fascinated me was the fact that the fish had continued to feed. Although big trout are often caught on bucktails or streamers, in *very* cold weather a nymph will outfish a minnowlike fly simply because the trout doesn't have to chase it through heavy currents. A nymph can be fished absolutely dead and catch fish, while a bucktail cannot; a nymph can also be fished alive when the accepted food form is otherwise dead. This is the ultimate conundrum.

I had some fabulous fishing in Montana last year during my annual fall trip. Western rivers are custom-made for the nymph artist, and some lakes produce big trout to no other method, except sporadically. Henrys Lake in Idaho is a classic example: here the trout gorge on green damselfly nymphs and also *Gammarus,* the so-called freshwater shrimp imitated by many nymph patterns. But the lake I have in mind is known for its voluminous mini-mayfly hatches where even the best dry-fly man can spook trout with a #22 on a 7X tippet. The naturals look like dandruff. There is some action at the beginning of an emergence, and you can hook three, maybe four nice fish. But the real sport occurs when the gulpers (fish of 4, 5, and 6 pounds) appear after rafts of spent mayflies are floating on the water. The fish cruise in a leisurely fashion, often porpoising in plain sight as they take ephemeral minutiae out of the surface film. With countless thousands of naturals windrowed to a small area, the most perfect imitation is lost in sheer numbers.

After we spent a futile Montana morning casting at repetitive risers and hooking exactly three trout, Tom McNally provided the solution. McNally, who is an expert angler in every sense of the word, learned nymphing fundamentals as a lad on the hard-fished streams of Maryland. He was also a pro boxer in his youth, and now shoots pool with Minnesota Fats, so he reacts to panic situations with sharply honed reflexes—in this case a #10 fuzzy-bodied brown nymph worked across the surface in a hand-twist retrieve. Absurd? Showing those trout something big and alive swimming through all those tiny inert mayflies commanded a gustatory response that had no equal.

The next morning we began hooking, with modest consistency, rainbows and browns in the 2½- to 4-pound class; these were hammered silver, deep-bodied, arrowheaded trout that leaped and rocketed off like bonefish.

Many simply popped our tippets, and we lost several large ones in the lake's numerous weed beds. This method of outfoxing the gulpers was no fluke. Tom and I visited that lake regularly through September and into aspen-yellow October. On any morning when the water was mirror calm his method paid off.

I enjoy writing about the joys of nymph fishing. It reminds me of Rube Cross. When I mentioned his book earlier, I had to go scrambling through my library to check the title. I remembered the volume had a brown cover, but I had forgotten that he wrote an inscription inside, and that told me the year I caught my first big trout. I visited his hayloft shop the following winter to learn more about tying flies. A huge man, half poet, half mountain lion, he was generous to a fault. His dill-pickle-size fingers spun the most beautiful flies I will ever see. But it's his inscription in my book that deserves to appear in print. The author remains anonymous, yet the words reflect to some degree the transcendental joy of angling:

> *To my young friend*
>
> *I dreamed,*
> *   that I again my native hills had found,*
> *the mossy rocks, the valley, and the*
> *   stream that used to hold me captive*
> *to its sound.*
> *And that I was a boy again.*
>
> *(Anon.)*

—REUBEN R. CROSS
January 3, 1937

Clinic

Today, there must be a hundred or more nymph patterns for every species of insect (and crustacean) consumed by trout. Don't be alarmed, however: You can get along with a dozen different colors and sizes—as a matter of fact, the Hare's Ear nymph alone seldom fails to take fish. While this may be an oversimplification of the art form, it's much more important for the beginner to first learn *how* to use the nymph.

You will need both a floating and a sinking-tip line; the floating line will take care of most nymphing situations from the surface down to 3 feet, while the sinking tip will send the fly much deeper, depending on the length of your cast and the speed of the current. With the floating line a 9- to 12-foot leader is most effective, but with the sinking tip a 6- to 7½-foot leader will send the nymph deeper and faster.

Nymphing is primarily a game of getting the fly to the level of feeding fish. At times, trout will take "emerger" nymphs directly on the surface, but on other occasions, especially in high, cold water, the fly must be worked slowly along the bottom. The ability to detect strikes from unseen fish (these may be no more than a slight pause or pull on the leader or the line) and to respond quickly are skills that must be developed with experience.

These nymph patterns are four old favorites that have taken many fine fish over the years. They suggest subaquatic food forms in general, and, except on those occasions when fish are truly selective, one or another will usually produce if worked at the right depth.

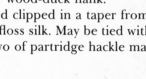

Strawman nymph

HOOK: Regular or 2XL in sizes to suit.
TAIL: A few strands of gray mallard or wood-duck flank.
BODY: Deerhair spun on hook thinly and clipped in a taper from tail to head, ribbed with pale yellow floss silk. May be tied without hackle or, if desired, a turn or two of partridge hackle may be added.

Hare's Ear nymph

HOOK: Regular shank, #6 to #16.
TAIL: Brown hackle.
BODY: Dubbed very rough with fur from European hare's ear, mixed with fur from the hare's face, ribbed with oval gold tinsel.
THORAX: Tied very full, with wing pad from gray goose or duck tied over.
LEGS: Dubbing from thorax picked out long and fuzzy; this represents the nymph legs.

Leadwing Coachman nymph

HOOK: #6 to #12, 2XL.
TAIL: Dark brown hackle feathers.
BODY: Bronze peacock herl ribbed with fine black silk.
HACKLE: Dark rusty brown.
WING PADS: Small dark black duck upper wing covert feathers (cut to shape).
HEAD: Brown lacquer.

Iron Blue nymph

HOOK: Regular shank, #6 to #16.
TAIL: Cream or gray hackle wisps.
BODY: Bluish muskrat ribbed with gold wire.
THORAX: Bluish muskrat, no rib.
HACKLE: Grayish cream.
HEAD: Clear lacquer over tying silk.

16

OF MICE AND MICKEYS

Any fishing that could keep Bert Lahr out of his tackle boxes had to be good. He always brought as many of them as he could squeeze into a boat, all Texas size. The moment he decided that fishing was slow, he withdrew from our world with monklike asceticism and studied his baits.

But things were different in Maine. Lahr never really had a chance to take inventory; smallmouth bass kept interrupting him. In fact, things were jumping in that watery hunk of real estate between routes 6 and 9. Maine anglers disdain this, but black-bass fans even now come half across the country to try the fishing in the hundred or so blue lakes that puncture Washington, Hancock, and Penobscot

counties. Twenty years ago Lahr and I had joined them
because it was June. The bass were on their beds, and one
didn't need a Ouija board to find them.

In the old days Maine fishing carried a men-only tag.
Nobody bathed or shaved for a week, and the camp got a
little gamey even before somebody put a bear cub in the
cook's bed. Now the plush bass-circuit resorts feature char-
coaled steaks, steamed lobsters, juicy rashers of smoked
bacon, and chowders that make my mouth water in the
remembering.

We stayed at Weatherby's Camp, which is still located
near the foot of Grand Lake. Bev Weatherby was an old-
style boniface, and he proudly stated that most of the other
operators in the area also run first-class layouts. You'll
usually find them represented in the advertising columns.
The point is, this is still an ideal area for a family fishing
trip. It's easy to get to, and the fishing remains first rate.

With so many waters to choose from, you will probably find your own favorite, as you would at home. It may
be a small lake, such as Horse Shoe, Norway, or Junior. Or
a large one, such as 17,219-acre Spednic or 11,520-acre
Big Lake. Or even others that can take a little extra time
to reach by boat. Famed or not, you come away with a
proprietary feeling. That's the way I remember one particular area, which Lahr said was the site of the greatest smallmouth fishing he'd ever had.

Before dawn one morning we left Weatherby's in two
canoes and motored eight miles across Grand Lake, then
down a great shining avenue called the Narrows into some
adjacent, smaller lakes. These waters are full of craggy
islets where sea birds nest, for the coast is not far away. Our
guide, Lew Brown, cut the motor at a vast rock bar, then
paddled very slowly just inside the dropoff. Lahr decided
to try his spinning rod while I cast a bug with my fly rod.

I don't remember how many fish we caught, nor is that

important. I know that one or the other of us had a bass
on most of the time. My old friend Bob Elliot was in a
second canoe with Creston MacArthur, casting along the
opposite side of the bar, and whenever I glanced that way
one of them was playing a fish. Our first bass ran a little
over a pound. Then for a while we hit a string of plump
2½-pounders. Lahr, with his spinner, was also catching an
occasional white perch or pickerel. The chainsides were
quite large, with 20- to 24-inch fish common. Well before
noon we had worked our way into the east arm and then
things really popped.

Of course, with a new lake in the offing, Lahr had to
find a new lure. Anyway, he was bored with the spinner.
Lew mentioned that artificial mice were dynamite here, so
Lahr opened a bait box about the size of a small steamer
trunk. "I got m-m-mice," he announced. "I'll s-s-slip the
bass a Mickey." He crouched over the box for a séance.
There were at least fifty imitation mice of all colors and
sizes joined in one hairy snarl. This would take time.

I lay out a popping bug along the bouldery shore and
before the ripples faded a beautiful smallmouth socked it.
My strike was slow. A few casts later I hooked a bass of
about 3 pounds, a perfect fish for lunch. I flipped it into the
canoe, intending to give it the coup de grace, but it flopped
wildly and landed smack in Lahr's open tackle box. He
stared at it a moment, then slammed the lid shut.

"These m-m-mices are fan-tastic!" he said.

Our lake on this day was 842 acres of crystal water
lying at the feet of forest-clad hills. It had every kind of bass
habitat that you could hope for: stumps, down timber, lily
beds, sloping shores, coves, shoals, points, boulders, and
gravelly islands. The thing that made it different for us was
the size of the fish and the fishing conditions. The bass had
finished spawning when we arrived and were surfacing
hungrily to a hatch of mayflies. I changed from my 9-foot

bugging rod to a featherweight 7-footer with a 3X leader and a #10 hairwing. The fish were cruising rapidly, so I had to place the fly at a point of interception. They'd streak like bronze arrows and hit the floater in a turn. It would be hard to find better fishing or a more acrobatic quarry.

Many 3-pound smallmouths provided action, plus an occasional one that scaled close to 4. The afternoon was a blur of jumping, zigzagging, diving fish, and they were still rising to the fly when the last rays of the sun lay a pearly mist across the birches. By the time we reached camp that evening my wrist was as stiff as a poker.

The smallmouth bass is a fly-rod fish par excellence. He develops guile and craftsmanship with age, and his solid weight against the spring of a rod as the reel sings shrilly to that first foaming rush is a pleasure to which no angler could be insensible. The bass runs, he doubles, he sulks, he leaps, he sounds, he goes under the boat; in fact, he does everything a gamefish is expected to do. Sometimes he looks like cloth of gold in the bright sun, but I have seen smallmouths of every color from glittering black to ruby-tinted. Maine fish are no pale carbon of the original, but a true bronze in most waters.

Smallmouths of 5 pounds are quite rare, because Northern bass populations do not have the long growing season of fish in the deep South. A lunker Maine smallmouth of over 4 pounds (and we took only three in two weeks) wouldn't raise an eyebrow in Tennessee. These days you have to hit 7 pounds to make a rebel yell. But a few ciphers of avoirdupois are meaningless to the real addict.

Anglers come from all over the country to the Maine ponds because the fishing is unique. For one thing, pressure is modest, even at the easily accessible resort ponds. Although Weatherby's Camp was at near capacity when we were there, we seldom saw other fishermen. That's because there are so many places to fish. And, of course, the down-easter scorns bass fishing as an eccentricity. A two-year survey of 1,358 anglers in the Big Lake region once disclosed that only 11—or less than 1 percent—were residents of Maine. So all the pressure is from the tourists, and that's far from intensive.

Some idea of the vast potential can be realized at Big Lake. Now, I don't rate it the best bass pond for fly fishing (there are anglers who will dispute that), but the Maine Fisheries Research and Management Division came up with some interesting facts about it that apply more or less to all lakes in the area. Of its 63 miles of shoreline, more than half is ideal for bass spawning. State biologists counted 4,218 nests, some only 12 feet apart.

This total, by the way, does not count beds on shallow gravelbars out in the lake, nor does it take into account the fact that many nests are used twice, by different breeders. It is conservatively estimated that each bed contributes to the annual fishery at least two bass that will live to be five years old. Actually, smallmouths can survive from 10 to 14 seasons. In all, there's one hell of a lot of bronzebacks to be caught, because 9 out of every 10 are released by anglers. The survey turned up one woman caster, evidently skillful, who had caught and released 70 bass up to 3½ pounds during an eight-hour period! That's good fishing in any country.

One day we hauled the canoes over to Wabassus Lake, 6 miles from camp. While Lew and Creston were unloading our gear I made a cast in a little stream that flows through a culvert under the roadway. A smallmouth hit the bug on the first cast. When I caught two more, Lahr got interested and began catching fish on a popping plug. Creston wanted to show off, so he came over with his double-jig rig and began taking them two at a time, making four doubles from one spot. There was no room for Lew, because this tableau was taking place in a pool about 20 yards across. "Nuts," said Lew. "Let's go where there's some *real* bass."

He had in mind the Wabassus inlet, which is controlled by a small dam. The water rushes into the lake swiftly and it's a natural collecting point for big smallmouths. We anchored on opposite sides of the broad current. Lahr hooked the first fish with a small diving plug, and a few seconds later a bass rolled into my popper as I let it swim over the froth. With the current to add power, our fish pinwheeled and streaked 20 yards before leaping again. It was a circus. We hooked and released about 50 bass before a storm rose.

I think an ideal combination for Maine smallmouths is a fly-rod outfit and a spinning or a baitcasting outfit. All bass-circuit ponds are excellent for fly fishing, because insects are a dominant food item. The Big Lake study revealed that insects are taken throughout the season and are particularly important in June, when dragonflies, damselflies, stoneflies, and mayflies are major food items. In August, the smallmouths consume three times more fish than insects, presumably because of their abundance, but by late September terrestrial insects, such as beetles, ants, and bees, are more to their liking.

So why two different kinds of tackle? Well, on stormy days when fly fishing becomes difficult, it's a relief to be able to switch to wind-cutting lures. I can cast a bug in anything short of a hurricane, but there are times when slopping waves make line handling a chore. Anglers who can't use a fly rod or a baitcasting rod will catch plenty of fish on spinning gear, using small wobbling spoons, spinners, jigs, and plugs. Bring along single-hook lures; they simplify turning bass loose.

The bass showed a degree of selectivity only on Norway and Big lakes. On a quiet afternoon we heard the

Norway bass working grassy margins of shore even before we located them. They were knocking fat, yellow mayfly subimagoes off the weed stems. We went to work, and any light-colored dry fly of the right size would bring an immediate strike. But they wouldn't hit a bug, and they spurned the dark dry patterns that had worked so well when we used them on Big Lake.

On Big Lake we'd found the bass cruising over open-water shoals for slaty black mayflies. They wanted something like a #14 Black Gnat—nothing else would do. Such moments, of course, add interest to the fishing. Bert Lahr, who, for all his deadpan clowning, really was an expert with the spin-stick, concluded that ¼- and ⅛-ounce spinners with yellow-and-white feathered skirts, worked slow and near the bottom, were the most reliable lures for large bass. Jigs ran a close second. Next came ¼-ounce darters and poppers in natural scale finishes.

Perhaps the most important factor in planning a Maine trip is the time. June is the best month for small-mouth bass—especially its two middle weeks. In a normal year, spawning is at its peak from about June 5 to June 20, and it guarantees fast fishing.

Take along light khaki clothing, for some days will be quite warm—but also be prepared for cold with wool shirts and wool jackets, because the weather can change overnight. Never go anywhere without rain gear. Early June in Maine is likely to be a rainy period, with storms coming up quickly.

There is very little stream fishing, and consequently no wading, so boots aren't necessary unless you want to spend a few hours casting for salmon. Lake trout and land-locks occur sporadically along the bass circuit. As in most areas, these salmonids are at their peak in the deep lakes right after ice-out, but they still offer some sport in mid-June. I don't care much for trolling, but Lahr dredged a

pair of 3-pound landlocks out of the Narrows one after-noon with a spoon. And although it was a bit late for salmon in Grand Lake Stream (which flows right by Weath-erby's Camp), I made it a ritual to wade the big pool below the dam every evening for an hour or so. Invariably I took three or four bouncing 18-inch landlocks on the dry fly. This was anticlimactic after a full day of smallmouth fishing, but then it's hard to put a rod away while there's still light on the water.

Clinic

Bert Lahr, the Cowardly Lion in *The Wizard of Oz,* has long gone to that eternal angling paradise, but *The Wizard* has captivated audiences ever since it was first screened in 1939. Bert was a very dear friend, and as unorthodox an angler as he was a comic. He was likely to use bass bugs to catch mackerel, or mackerel jigs to catch bass. One of his favorite rigs for smallmouths was the double jig, which consists of a ¼-ounce lead-head at the terminal end, and a ⅛-ounce or smaller jig tied in with a perfection loop knot about 3 feet up the monofilament line (the loop is formed first as the tag end must be free to complete the knot). During "hot" periods when bass were active this often resulted in a doubleheader, not always two bass but often a chain pickerel, or a pair of perch. One day on a Manitoba lake with Tom and Bob McNally, we were about to have a fishless lunch when a school of whitefish began rising near shore. A hastily made double jig rig produced three double-headers before the cook fire was aglow. The reason for the heavier jig at the terminal end is to prevent aerial twisting or tangling during the cast. It is also a good way to deliver a really small jig over a long distance.

Double-jig rig

17

AN ANCIENT ART REVISITED

I would rather catch a trout on a dry fly than any other way, because I like to see the fish rise and splash. But there are very few days on our local streams when surface fishing is profitable. An honest Catskill trout would have to scratch his head to remember when he last saw a Green Drake. Now, there are rivers in America where trout come regularly to the dry fly, and I have waded many of them. But good dry-fly streams are the exception rather than the rule, and if the truth be known, the average man is lucky when he gets a dozen top-water sessions in one season. Another thing that works against the dry-fly caster is the fact that large fish are not fond of poking their heads at the surface except under unusual conditions. High-caste brahmins have stressed the sporting aspects of top-water fishing ever since the turn of the century, and in the course of extolling it, they shrank from the black riddle of how to improve our most ancient art—the wet, or sunken, fly.

The Meadows stretch of the upper Housatonic River in Connecticut is a big, mean stream, big as the Eel in California and rough as the McKenzie in Oregon if you wade the wrong places. The slab rock and boulder bottom give a deceptive yellowish tinge to the water, and no matter how deep you might think the next pothole is, it's always a few feet deeper. My fishing record on the Housatonic during the late 1940s was absurd. I had caught fewer trout here than anyplace, and it was some time before I could thumb through my lengthy catalog of misery filed under Connecticut and find a figure noted in the catch column.

The tricky thing is that wet-fly work divides itself into two distinct phases on heavy rivers such as the Housatonic —a two-fly or preferably three-fly cast skittered on the surface during the early season, and a single wet fly on the long drift for late-season fishing. The three-fly cast requires a balanced leader to keep a trio of #6s from tangling, and the single-fly cast demands a long, fine leader if a #12 is to be teased near the stream bottom.

I want to make this stratagem clear from the outset, because terminal tackle makes a great difference in results. A long, light leader is necessary when the stream drops clear, not only because of its near invisibility but also because it allows a fly to drift and turn like a natural insect. In my opinion, the leader is even more important than the choice of fly pattern, yet the majority of leaders in use today are totally inadequate for lifelike presentation. The tippet section must be long and fine so that the fly will sink fast with a minimum of disturbance. A short or heavy tippet will simply hold the wet fly rigid, and unless the whole leader is properly tapered, it won't sink. I use two different profiles in making leaders—a single-fly design, which allows free movement of the feathers even in the faintest current, and a three-fly design, which casts on a short line without fouling. Although I don't promise any magical properties in the fly patterns I recommend, the leaders will definitely increase your score. The one-fly leader will follow every whim of the current, and to late-season fish that is important. With a three-fly cast in the high, rough water of early season, natural drifting is unnecessary, and the leader need only support the flies.

According to my notebook, the best period for the three-fly cast has been from late April through the month of June. Take a day when the river is flowing full, with some insect activity but no rising fish, and you have the makings of a real wet-fly session. Short casts across stream and downstream drifting into probable trout holds are most effective, but the speed of the retrieve should be adjusted according to the character of the water. In the turbulent runs of the Housatonic, I often used nothing but #6s this past spring, holding as much line as possible off the surface and fluttering the flies in a swimming movement, using a fast rod rhythm to keep them alive. For the first time, some really nice fish came boiling out of the river. In slower reaches, I had to tone down the action of the flies, drawing them back at a speed comparable to the current. By early June, my catches fell off badly. As the trout got fatter and more selective, I went to smaller flies, and finally to the single wet fly on a long drift. A one-fly cast lasted me through the summer and between those brief periods when fly hatches made surface fishing worthwhile. We had one three-week period when the river ran without a dimple, day after day. This is a compressed case history, and actually the story began a good many years ago.

There was a day on the North Branch of the Au Sable

in Michigan when fishing was kind of slow. In fact, it was as dull as spinach, and the best I could muster was two smallish trout. Arriving at the concrete bridge, I clambered out of the river to rest, when I saw three trout lying upstream, each a good distance apart. The fish held low in the water, for when surface feed is scarce they must take a broader view of the stream. The closer a fish comes to the top, the smaller his cone of vision becomes, which is one reason why we often have less difficulty catching a trout when he's busy working on the surface. I don't remember what fly was secure to my leader, but the leader was a standard 7½-foot trout size. After a few minutes' wait, I slipped in below the nearest fish and placed the fly across and upstream so that it would swim near him with the fly just under the surface. After two drifts, the trout sank out of sight. I had put him down.

My next fish was a smaller one, and although the cast was nearly perfect, he glided to the bottom almost immediately after the fly touched the water. This was not the way I expected an obviously anxious trout to behave. It seemed proper to select a new fly before approaching a third fish, but I had been changing flies all morning and, rather than lose face in my growing belief that the pattern was unimportant, I changed leaders. I tied on a 9-foot leader, and (before you become paralyzed by skepticism) the third trout took a casual look at the fly and departed. Graveled by this turn of events, I quickly added bits and pieces of leader material, and, since each new failure multiplied the occasions for lengthening it, the leader finally outran my capacity to cope with it. When I put a sixth fish down, the end product was no less than 15 feet long, and all I had accomplished was to project the old losing race on a gigantic scale.

The analysis of an angling problem is always based on the assumption that fish are entirely predictable. This, I beg to point out, cannot possibly be the case. The day was getting late, so the only logical course was to fish back downstream toward camp, arriving in time for supper. I didn't wade too far before a good trout took hold; then two more made flashing passes at the fly before I reached the bridge. Just below the bridge I picked up another brownie and a small rainbow. In the long glide below, three more trout struck. None of these fish weighed more than a pound, but epoch-making events often rest on a slender pivot. The problem had crumbled to an ash when I touched it. By fishing across and downstream, I achieved long, quiet drifts with the fly, and, in the deadly flat water of the North Branch, the slightest disturbance was enough to send summer trout running for cover. Had they been surface feeding, holding a few inches under the water, my line might not have broken their window of vision. So here, for the first time, I saw the relationship between a trout's feeding level and possible methods of presentation.

The method was essentially simple. I cast the fly almost directly across stream, following the drift of the line with my rod tip, then paying out slack as the line commenced to tighten. When the drift had covered a wide reach, I made a very slow retrieve, imparting just the slightest swimming movement to the fly.

Upstream casting should theoretically be more effective in flat water, because the angler can approach his trout more closely from behind; but sun and water are tricky factors, and the handiest empirical proof can be found in our empty creels. I would much prefer dropping my front taper 20 feet away from a near-surface trout, letting the fly swim into his field of vision, than make a "perfect" upstream throw which literally puts the line in the fish's eye.

It is barely possible that with a properly designed leader my fish on the North Branch could have been taken on an upstream cast. I followed the very ancient formula of leader making in those days, which was, simply stated, thick butt, fine tippet, and graduated strands in between. The results, of course, were never predictable. My line point was too heavy, because a very skilled Au Sable angler told me so, and, combined with a straight-taper leader, my terminal tackle left much to be desired. Upstream casting is a refined method of wet-fly fishing, extremely deadly at times, but on the whole not nearly so urgent as early pioneers have made it out to be. To narrow the field down, I'd mark upstream casts essential to nymph fishing for the very good reason that nymphing is an attempt at exact imitation, whereas wet-fly fishing is an art of suggestion. Many of the most popular wet-fly patterns are as improbable in the world of insects as a Mau Mau in Manhattan.

There are a number of wet-fly patterns that will take
fish anywhere, possibly not as deftly as some local favorite,
but, for the average angler buying a basic assortment, the
Leadwing Coachman, Iron Blue Dun, Ginger Quill, March
Brown, Gold-Ribbed Hare's Ear, Gray Hackle Yellow,
Light Cahill, Royal Coachman, Professor, Cowdung (with
picked olive seal-fur body), Grizzly King, and something
flashy—say, a Silver Doctor, or Campbell's Fancy—would
make a valuable dozen to start with. These patterns are old
and reliable. It is wise to have buggy-looking sunk patterns
as well as the flashier type; bright-tinseled patterns usually
work best on cold days when the wind is blowing a bag in
your line. They can be worked fast because, unlike dull-
colored flies which might pass for the larval forms of insects, the fancy patterns undoubtedly simulate small minnows. There is no set rule, of course, as the speed of
retrieve depends on existing conditions. For the three-fly
cast, you should use a white-winged pattern, such as the
Royal Coachman, on the top dropper to help in locating
the position of all three flies.

Whether the line should sink or float depends to a
great extent on how deep you have to fish. Most talented
lake casters are partial to a sunken line. Maine and Quebec
are big wet-fly consumers because their pond trout usually
forage well under the surface and you can't get near them
without dipping your line point. On the other hand, deep
fishing is not necessary in lakes where the surface waters
remain cold through the summer, such as high altitude
waters in the Rockies and British Columbia. Here you can
float the line and have the advantage of "seeing" the strike.
Stream fishermen, of course, are faced with the problem of
regulating the depth of the fly, and in really big rivers a
partly submerged line might be necessary. Whenever possible, I try to avoid sinking my line because of drag and
because strikes are harder to detect.

The knack of hooking a fish with wet flies comes through experience, and it is very difficult to tell anyone how to do it. In upstream casting, for instance, you have to develop the ability to cast a fairly straight line, and at the same time keep enough slack in your leader to permit the fly to drift naturally. In downstream casting, the trout will hit so fast that the beginner is apt to miss completely, or strike too hard.

I have met wet-fly experts the world over, but I think the most highly specialized angler was a chap I watched at work on the Mangfall River in Bavaria. There was a long, deep place where the river broke in two, the smaller part bubbling off through a meadow and the larger part running into an embankment of stone where silvery grayling poised on the edge of the shadows to rise and dip in the current like kites on a string. Where the two parts joined again, the river spilled into a hissing waterfall which showered over a great sapphire-blue pool. Perched like a colorful birdhouse on the hill above was the Zum Froehlichen Forelle—the "Inn of the Playful Trout." As a rule, innkeepers who conduct their business on trout streams are inclined to regard anglers as moony eccentrics, but this fellow was more ardent than his customers. Every evening after supper he would bolt for a choice gravelbar in the big pool while his guests were still getting into their waders.

His rod was 10½ feet long, very supple, and obviously designed solely for wet-fly fishing. For a line he used an IFI, probably of British make, and a 12-foot leader. One small Grouse and Green wet fly completed his rig, and I must say that under the conditions that existed this outfit was absolutely ideal. He would work the pool very slowly from head to tail, making short cross-stream casts and gradually lengthening them to cover the width of the river. Perhaps the easiest way to describe his method is to say that the fly was fished the way we would drift live bait—a worm or a minnow. Most of the light line sank and his long, fine leader moved very slowly through the water, so slowly that I wondered at first if he were using a fly at all.

Trout fishing was always good on the Mangfall, but nobody ever caught as many large fish as the keeper at the Inn of the Playful Trout. The man knew the mood of his river and the temperament of its inhabitants. I believe that most of us can profit by his example.

The leader profiles illustrated at the end of this chapter are for nylon, and their diameters are given in thousandths of an inch. The pound-test system of material classification has too much variation to be practical. A .007-inch tippet might be anywhere from 4-pound-test to 7-pound-test, and in the larger sizes, from .010 up, variations are even greater. Inasmuch as a well-balanced leader is dependent on its taper, the only important factor is thickness, not strength. Several manufacturers make nylon diameters known on the spool or package, and any smart tackle shop operator will have a micrometer or thickness gauge on hand, so you shouldn't have any difficulty getting the correct sizes. I realize that many wet-fly fishermen still use level leaders, but there's no doubt in my mind that a season's trial of the tapered kind will demonstrate its superiority, both in casting and fishing the fly.

Clinic

Formulas for leader profiles are legion and, indeed, you can simply buy an over-the-counter tapered leader of the desired length and give it no further thought. However, I am seldom satisfied with commercial concepts and find myself cutting off or adding sections to get just the right turnover and a lifelike swim in the fly. The profiles illustrated here for the single-fly and the three-fly cast are eminently practical. Fishing with three flies is an ancient ploy, virtually unutilized by modern anglers, but in big turbulent rivers such as the Madison or Delaware the rig is as effective today as it was in the era of the greenheart rod. The dropper strands are formed by leaving a 6-inch tag end of monofilament when the blood knot is made. The top dropper or "dancing" fly often triggers strikes when skittered on the surface during the retrieve.

9½-foot leader

18"	16"	20"	20"	40"
of	of	of	of	of
.015	.012	.010	.009	.007

9-foot leader

32"	32"	12"	12"	20"
of	of	of	of	of
.016	.014	.012	.010	.008

Leader design

At this time of writing, braided butt-leaders have been introduced to the market and, after limited use, it would appear that these are a trade-off in substituting mass for stiffness in their multistrand butts or "collars." As yet, I don't see any particular advantage in this type of leader. Only time will tell.

18

A TWITCH IN TIME

At times drag can be put to good advantage. Drag, in case you're a beginning fly fisherman, is that condition that causes a dry fly to kick up a little wake and go skimming across the surface. The fly gets its speed from the line which is caught in faster currents, thus pulling the fly along. This is seldom attractive to a trout. As a matter of fact, a dragging fly and line will generally send the fish diving for cover. So the dry-fly fisherman casts his feathers upstream, putting enough slack in the cast to get a natural drift. With the line floating back toward the angler, he can make the necessary adjustments with his rod to keep the line from bellying in the current. If he were to face downstream and cast, the line would tighten up almost immediately. This is so difficult to prevent that few people ever turn around.

We know, too, that trout always rest with their heads facing upstream, and that consequently the easiest way to stalk them is by facing the same direction and coming up from behind. The angler can get nearer his quarry, hook it more easily, and play it in water that has already been covered. With this weight in favor of upstream casting, dry-fly fishing is resolved to a simple formula. Yet the dry fly downstream can be a deadly method at times, and, if executed properly, will take large trout from spots that would otherwise go untouched.

Late one afternoon, on the Willowemoc River, I waded into a stretch of water that squeezed between high, brush-covered banks. At the head of the riffle, a string of piano-size boulders straddled the streambed, so I began by testing the deep pockets around each rock. On the far bank, a dark eddy swept in behind one boulder, and above this bare dome a fat hemlock dropped a screen of branches to the water—blocking any casts from a downstream or across stream position. I walked a short distance above the eddy to where a gravelbar sloped out into the river and, by wading carefully, I managed to flip a bucktail into the quiet parts around the hemlock sweeper. It was like casting into a tunnel. On the first toss, a trout flashed behind the fly. On the second cast he moved away from the fly and took a position over a patch of white pebbles next to the boulder.

I tried a smaller bucktail on the next cast, and then a wet fly which only succeeded in flushing a small brook trout. The native came speeding straight upstream and wiggled under a rock almost at my feet. Nothing seemed to interest or disturb the fat brown trout lying next to the boulder, however; he lay there with his white mouth opening and closing. I didn't bother to cast anymore, but instead sat on a half-submerged boulder, wondering what to do next. The idea of floating a dry fly over his head occurred to me, but it took the trout to lend encouragement.

I saw the fish rise about 40 feet below me; his sharp head broke the surface and slid gently out of sight. I worked out my cast until there was just enough line to fall 5 or 6 feet short of his position and then, with an abrupt check, the bivisible fell to the water and drifted slowly over his lair. The trout crossed the patch of white pebbles and moved slowly behind the fly. Several times he made feeble passes at it, never quite making up his mind. Time was running out. I kept lengthening the drift with slack, and now the fly began moving faster toward the tail of the eddy and suddenly the fish turned, facing upstream. I stopped the slack and raised my rod tip, skidding the bivisible right back over his head. That movement of the fly was like touching off a shotgun. The trout took the fly instantly, and made a surface-churning run straight downstream. Had the fish been less ambitious, a few turns around the hemlock branches would have been an easy out.

After netting the fish I walked back up to the hemlock and spent a few minutes examining the branches. It was no surprise to find three different pieces of leader hanging there. In all probability the sweeper was good for 30 more. On a hard-fished Catskill stream, you don't find sizable trout in places that are easily covered. This lair was probably bypassed a hundred times in the course of a season.

The parachute cast is the best way to drop a fly downstream. Line and leader will stretch out and fall slack, just slack enough to give you a long drift without paying out too much line. Most important is that the slack is not concentrated in one big belly of line—but *distributed* throughout its floating length. When slack is concentrated in one area, too much line is exposed broadside to the current and drag starts almost immediately. If you want to reach a fish that is out of range, make a cast downstream, and by shaking line out, the additional floating slack will carry the fly out. The parachute cast is not only useful downstream, but across currents of varying speeds as well.

To execute the parachute cast, you false-cast in the usual manner, holding the rod and line higher than usual until the required length is obtained on the last cast. On the forward drive, stop the rod at *vertical*, simultaneously lowering the rod hand about 18 inches; this abrupt stop will pull the leader and line back, while the lowering of the rod drops it to the water in the same position as it was checked. This differs from the ordinary slack-line cast in which the angler lengthens his line until it extends a few feet beyond the target—at which point he checks the forward cast, simultaneously lowering his rod *tip*. The result

of the latter is wide elbows of slack which are difficult to control.

For downstream casting I like to use small, stiff-hackled bivisibles. They not only float well, but on a calm surface their wake is hardly noticeable. A heavy-hackled fly is apt to kick up too much disturbance and put the fish down. I don't think pattern is as important in this type of fishing. A gray, black, or brown bivisible—depending on which you can see the best—will usually bring a trout to the top if he's going to come at all. Flies tied with a wide hackle at the eye skip over the water better than those bivisibles of almost uniform diameter, which unfortunately are in the majority. The longer hackle at the eye causes the fly to tip forward, keeping the hook in the air. After a little experimentation you'll find quite a difference in the working qualities of various designs.

There's a subtle distinction between a "worked" fly and a dragging fly. To clear this up: A worked fly is one that is moving (in this case on the surface) against the current in short, pulsing strokes bearing a fleeting resemblance to some strong-winged insect who wants to go upstream. For what reason I can't imagine. Whereas a dragging fly is less artfully played, the lure making a broad wake and bearing a complete resemblance to a Royal Coachman. Why one man can work his lure and the other can only drag it is as elusive a question as why one man can paint and the other cannot. Judging from the anglers I have watched who can bring a husky brown trout boiling into a worked floater, a highly developed fish sense is essential. I do know that heavy-bellied fly lines and heavy-hooked flies are no asset upstream or down. To get the best results the leader should be as long as possible.

The complete downstream technique consists of letting the dry fly drift on a slack line until you've covered the holding water, and then bringing the fly back upstream in short, darting strokes. It's a good idea to make the fly dart with some authority—don't let the feathers hang in the current like a wet mop. The natural drift downstream will give the fish a chance to rise to a slack cast if he's so inclined—but retrieve with a teasing jumping motion by flexing your wrist and slowly raising the rod tip. If the fish rises and follows the fly while it's drifting freely, keep playing slack out to the very last moment; but if he rejects the fly, stop the drift before the line passes over him. These suggestions are simply commonsense fishing. In any given situation you'll have to adjust the length of drift to the reaction of the fish—provided you see him.

If there's no fish in sight you'll have to rely on your knowledge of trout habits and cover the holding water as if you knew the fish was there. Such situations are in the minority, however, as the usual reason for turning around is to cover a fish who wouldn't play ball on the upstream field. On rare occasions you might want to try a complete reverse when things are slow, and in that event simply follow the drift-and-work routine, making a minimum of casts and working each for a maximum time on the water.

Many years ago, on the upper Campbell River, I fished down through a stretch of rough water which tumbled over a small fall into a broad, flat pool. It had been perfect wet-fly water up to this point, but the trout were uniformly small, a condition not uncommon in isolated sections of bedrock rivers. Trout food can't thrive on bare, current-swept rock. But this giant basin of clear water had a good gravel bottom and, as I expected, big cutthroats were showing at the surface. I walked along the shore studying the gravelbars that sloped into the river. One bar, which dipped off a small island, bisected most of the pool, so I waded out 30 or 40 yards and stopped for a cigarette. The water was so clear that every stone sparkled like a jewel. Three or four fish were working out of range, but just before I finished my smoke they had drifted into reach.

In the wilderness of Vancouver Island you wouldn't expect a trout to be suspicious. These trout were not suspicious—they were downright incredulous. The larger fish foraged by himself, tipping up and down, sucking in caddisflies as the slow current drifted him along. My casts were beautiful. The little fly sat quietly on the water and drifted almost into the trout's mouth time and again, but the damfool fish just ignored it. I covered the lesser trout just as neatly and got the same response. It wasn't until the trio had drifted downstream from me that the fun began.

The first parachute cast didn't get a glance on the slack drift, but a few twitches on the dragging fly brought the big cutthroat roaring into the feathers. There began one of the busiest days fishing I've ever had. Bill MacDonald, then fishing editor of *Forest and Outdoors,* joined me later that afternoon, and between the two of us we landed an estimated 60 trout up to 4 pounds in weight.

Black bass and Atlantic salmon will both hit a worked dry fly. As a matter of fact, they will hit a dragging dry fly as often as not, and consequently there's no novelty in fishing them downstream. Trout are more cautious feeders, however; the brook trout less so than the rainbow, and the rainbow less so than the brown. This difference within the trout family has been proven time and again in controlled scientific research projects. I cite this in passing simply to point out that statistics seem to bear out my observations on the attitude of each trout species about taking a fly fished in any manner.

There are definitely times when a "worked" dry fly will take trout while the orthodox upstream, drag-free cast will not. I paid particular attention to this in my trout fishing during the 1950 season, to get positive ideas for my column. As with most other anglers, my downstream dry-fly fishing had been more of an emergency measure than a technique. We know, of course, that on many white-water Western rivers, downstream dry-fly fishing is the *only* technique. The boiling riffles of the McKenzie in Oregon, for instance, are fished in no other way. A large, bushy dry fly is tossed in likely places and skipped back over the surface —without even bothering to cover the water with a slack drift first. The surface is so broken that drag doesn't matter in the least. The same technique isn't as successful in flat water, nor in Midwestern and Eastern rivers where brown trout predominate. But the parachute cast seems to satisfy a good percentage of the flat-water fish, and I think the reason is fairly obvious. Assuming that the slack drift rides over a trout without showing any line, it's reasonable to allow that some interest was aroused in this "natural" float —and when the fly does come to life, by darting against the current, our victim (who has had his eye on it) responds with little suspicion. This is a far cry from slapping out a cast that drags over the fish from the moment it hits the water.

One early and most convincing incident occurred on the upper Housatonic River more than thirty years ago. The Meadows is still restricted to fly fishing only, and consequently some walloping big brown trout live in this broad water. A daily rise and fall in water level due to the opening and closing of the dam allows just a few fishing hours in the morning and evening.

Trout were dimpling the surface all around me and the best I could manage was one smallish brownie during the first hour. A long black fish lay in a riffle making those head and tail rises that mark the wise one. Determined to do him in, I cast and cast, stopping only to change flies. At one point I looked over my shoulder to check a sloppy back cast, and saw a trout just as heavy as the first one—going through the same motions. In an instant I did an about-face and shortened my line, parachuting a cast right down his alley. The trout actually came to the drift and turned away, but when the fly started to dart over him he pulled it under the surface with a small tug. There was just enough light left to go back and try for the other fish, and suffice it to say the worked fly worked again.

You cannot reasonably expect to get your best dry-fly fishing by fishing downstream all day. For the many reasons pointed out earlier in this chapter, casting upstream is certainly more effective. The parachute cast, however, is of infinite value over rising trout, and for covering water that cannot be reached from a downstream position. On days when nothing seems to be moving fish it certainly pays to reverse the field and stir them up. Even on placid chalk-streams, where a moving fly is avoided like the plague, a worked fly has brought smashing strikes. Remember, until the year 1846 it was considered heresy to cast upstream, and, in the transition to dry-fly fishing during the years following, none but the dour wet-fly fisherman continued to wade with the current. I think much of the dry-fly art was lost by this one-track-mindedness.

Clinic

The parachute cast mentioned in this chapter is a cast in which the line does not fall straight on the water but instead drops in a series of slack curves, so that by the time the line has been straightened out by the current and drag

begins, the fly has already drifted some distance in a natural float. With the parachute cast, this is accomplished by
overpowering an ordinary forward cast and abruptly
checking the rod as shown. The line will kick backward and
fall to the surface in loose S shapes. If your objective is also
to put drag-reducing slack in a long leader tippet, the
parachute cast will accomplish this better than the lazy-S
cast, as described in chapter 14. After making this cast, it's

Parachute cast

important to bring your rod tip down close to the surface in order to tighten the line quickly at a striking fish. Once the line straightens in the current, raise your tip once again to near-vertical, minimizing the length of line on the water to get a lifelike swim of the fly.

19

LARGE THOUGHTS ON SMALL STREAMS

Periodically, I get an overpowering urge to visit a certain small trout stream that has miraculously escaped bulldozers, dam builders, housing developments, irrigation projects, and the assorted ills of modern society. It's about as rare as a Ming vase. My collection of miniature rivers is rapidly dwindling, but this one has remained virtually unchanged since I first fished it—almost fifty years ago. I've never caught a really large trout out of it, and I doubt if it ever holds a fish of much over 3 pounds. Yet I wouldn't trade one day here for equal time on the world's most fabled rivers. I always come home realizing what a clumsy fisherman I am and feeling immensely grateful for any minor triumphs. Trying to fly cast to places that would give a squirrel claustrophobia while eyeball-to-eyeball with a wild trout is a kind of mania that my wife Patti not only tolerates but obviously enjoys. The hand that rocks the cradle becomes the paw of a grizzly when she's turned loose in trout country.

There are several deep holes in the stream that are more than a hundred feet in width; one is far up on the mountain below a waterfall, the next at a covered bridge, and the last at a picnic ground. However, most of the stream is less than 20 feet wide, and to keep from scaring each other's fish we alternate sections so that we meet at the bridge for a sandwich and arrive at the waterfall by evening. On this particular day, I left Patti at her favorite run behind the church, or what used to be a church until the preacher abandoned his parish during the Great Depression. Nevertheless, Patti religiously tiptoes to the Church Pool as though she's about to discover the Holy Grail. A few years ago she caught an 18½-inch rainbow in its bubbly currents—which has excluded *me* from ever laying a feather on it.

Patti made a final check of her shoulder sack. I won't describe the junk she carries, but *some* of it is fishing tackle.

"Oh, you better gimme more watchamacallits." (This is a Letort Beetle, which isn't worth beans here, but she always finds some village idiot who eats watchamacallits. I buy them, recognizing her addiction.)

"Here's a fresh dozen."

"Good-bye," she said and dashed off.

I wandered up the brook past ramparts of blackberry brambles tangled in that uncaring growth of August, loud with the hum of bees and the dry rustle of thrushes. Probing the greeny pockets ahead, I hooked a trout now and then, colorful little jewels that sparkled and danced in the sunshine. From experience I knew that there would be no "big" fish until I reached the dense forest where moss and fern-fringed pools formed glassy steps down the mountainside. The vague promise of a 15-inch-long trout made my pace both anxious and careless. I splashed through a shallow ford where the amber stones are spread out like a gravel driveway—not even bothering to reconnoiter the area—when a fat brownie of at least a pound in weight literally shot out from under my feet. I should have known better. Trout of little rivers are opportunists, often foraging in places where there is no shelter but an abundance of food. I caught a 21-inch cutthroat recently in a small Western stream from the inside edge of a cress bed where the fish was rooting with its back out of the water. From a distance, it looked like a muskrat.

My shirt was streaked with sweat by the time I reached the tree line. I heard five or six grouse take off one after the other. A comforting sound. Nobody was fishing the water above. I could smell the cold spring seepage that drained from both banks—as heady as the aroma of autumn grapes bursting on the vine. I removed my steamed Polaroids and entered a darkening forest. The shallow tail of Fiddlehead Pool looked barren at first. A brisk breeze tossed the hemlock tops and a midday sun blinked from the surface like a giant signal mirror. Two or three minutes passed before I saw a dimpling rise.

The fish was plainly visible between sun flashes, balanced on enameled fins, swaying from side to side, on the watch for hapless insects that rafted into the narrowing current. I walked slowly along the bank to a place where there was room for a backcast, keeping my eyes on the fish —all the while crouching lower and lower until I was kneeling on the gravel in 6 inches of water. I felt a chill trickle into my right boot. My belt loop had slipped. The trout rose not once, but twice, in quick bubbly turns.

I swished the little bamboo pole back and forth, wait-

ing to feel the tug of line, only to discover that the leader
knot, so perfectly nailed, was stuck in a snake guide. Squat-
ting there, I pulled at the leader, but my rod tip bent
alarmingly.

Afraid to stand and be seen by the trout, I eased the
rod butt behind me and groped like a blind man for the tip,
still watching my quarry for any sign of alarm. The fish rose
again in a confident *slurp*. Water poured in both boots as
I sat backward on my heels and freed the leader knot.

A kingfisher came *scree*ing up the brook and lit on a
hemlock branch to study me along the arrow of its beak.
Evidently the trout was too big to interest *him*, but all I
could think of now was to get the fly in front of that fish.
I began waving the rod again, and after I clipped a fringe
of hemlock on the second back cast and corrected its speed
on the third, the line shot out in a gravity-defying roll and

fell gently to the water. Jon Tarantino would have been envious.

The trout never hesitated. It ran like hell upstream leaving a wake that lapped both shores.

An IBM computer isn't brain enough to count all the trout I never caught, nor could a team of double-domed experts feed it enough information to explain why. One is tempted to say that the fish saw the line at the last instant, which may be the case, or it saw the flash of the leader— or more likely by some uncanny instinct the trout knew I was skulking about and simply waited for a hostile gesture before going.

For the next half mile I worked a tricky section where short riffles zigzag from one bank to the other. In the springtime the area is scoured by floods which deposit dead limbs and leaf mats in every shallow place. Despite a thinness of flow, it's always worth exploring, as new pockets form each season, and they generally hold a few nice trout. In my early years, I lost a great many flies here, not to violent fish but by getting snagged in the debris.

Ordinarily when I'm dry-fly fishing I use the roll pickup. This is nothing more than an unfinished roll cast in which I snap the tip downward to lift the line, then pick the fly out of the air and go into a regular backcast. When fishing with a sunken fly line, using nymphs and wet patterns, I make a short left-hand pull to raise and move the line toward me before making the backcast. I also use the pull followed by a straight lift when casting a very long line, or in places where there's no likelihood of taking fish close to the rod. I suppose these methods are the most commonly used. However, in small streams, where most of your casting is done in knee-deep water, you will often be working pockets 30 feet away while most of your line is drifting around stones, branches, and other obstacles. Making an ordinary pickup or even a roll is difficult, because the line continually snags when drawn *across* the surface.

Obviously, a pickup that lifts line *upward* from the water will escape getting hung. The snap pickup solves that problem. The fly literally jumps out of the debris. The snap pickup has the further advantage of permitting you to work the fly right up to your boots. It doesn't make any difference about the slack between tip and fly, even if a fish hits, because one quick wrist movement will set the hook.

Essentially, the snap pickup consists of nothing more than raising your rod from a 10- to an 11-o'clock position, then snapping the tip back to 10 o'clock. The snap motion forms a moving curve that instantly runs down to the leader, lifting line off the water—and *flip*, your taper is airborne. I make my normal backcast just at the point when the leader clears the surface. You might be a bit splashy on the first few attempts because there's a tendency to use too much power or use it at the wrong angle. But when the snap pickup is done correctly, there is no splash and the fly flicks off the water as if by magic. The same snap movement will set the hook if a fish follows and takes the fly at the last instant.

The great fascination of small-stream fly fishing is that you invariably see your trout. Maybe he will be rolling head and tail under a hemlock bough or feinting left and right in the rippling places around a boulder, but his stance shows that he is more interested in looking at a new fly than contemplating the last one. Of course you aren't admitted to this heady intimacy while standing upright. Nothing spooks a trout quicker than the sight of a man. A deer, a cow, even an otter can amble along the brook with impunity; you cannot. Peek through the alders or stub your toe and you create havoc. But crawl along the brook as if you're looking for a lost collar button and the trout won't give you a tumble.

The distance at which a trout can see you varies considerably. I've given up trying to understand the "window" theory of trout vision because I can spook fish even when I'm flat on my belly below its incredible 97.6-degree field of view. (God knows who measured *this,* but it should make you keep your head down, anyhow.) The only sensible approach upon locating a trout is to stalk from a position just as close to the ground or water as you can possibly manage. If there is any natural cover, take advantage of it. Rather than be silhouetted against the sky, creep, crawl, hide behind a tree or boulder, and throw a low line.

There's a run above the covered bridge that is a real challenge. After Patti and I ate our sandwiches (she had taken a nice brook trout of about 14 inches) I decided to try Mud Bend. This is my exercise in total frustration. A deeply sedimented branch off the main stream, it's cold as ice, rooted with cress beds, and loaded with trout. But the banks are so completely overgrown that the only tactic I've ever been able to devise is to step in the water and slowly sink to a comfortable level, then hope the fish will start rising again. There are overhead tunnels among the hemlocks, and if I can find a trout lying in juxtaposition to one and make a perfect backcast, I might score. This requires double hauling at top speed to unroll a tight loop between the limbs. I always do this waiting to hear my rod tip splinter—but with 6X or 7X tippet, the leader, in theory, pops first.

My pants were already soaked, so I eased out into the stream and settled knee-deep into the muck. The water lapped at my boot tops. There were a few trout rising and amazingly my entrance didn't put them down. One greedy fish, just beyond casting range, was making a real commotion cruising back and forth under a cloud of caddisflies. I waited an eternity, hoping he'd move closer. Then the trout stopped feeding and disappeared. *Nuts.* Patti passed by.

"You look like you sank."

"I did."

"Can't you get out?"

"I don't want to. I'm waiting for a fish."

"Why don't you wait on the bank?"

"For the luva Pete's sake be *quiet*. This is a tactical position."

"Oh," she whispered, "I just wanted to borrow more watchamacallits. The fish chewed mine up. But I'll use something else. Don't catch cold." She disappeared in the brush.

By this time I decided that casting was better than freezing to death, so I teased out a low line foot by foot and, feeling a responding arc in the rod, I changed planes, hauling the line high in a hemlock tunnel. A miracle. Nothing went wrong. The line shot out and the leader straightened with a *bang* as a beautiful hammered-silver rainbow turned end over end. The trout ripped past me and for the next ten minutes he raced up and down Mud Bend. I didn't even try to unhook him properly. My legs were absolutely immobilized and there was no shallow where I could calm him down. The fish was too quick and lively to grip without injuring his plumbing, so I eased my fingers along the tippet and snapped it at the fly. He would wear it like an honor badge—for a short time anyhow. I gave myself 16 inches of credit, then gently tossed my rod on the bank and pulled myself out of the muck by hugging the nearest tree.

When I reached the waterfall, all I could see of Patti was her blond head bobbing among the rhododendron. Every so often her line would fall through the air like a frail cobweb against the purpling hemlocks. Somehow it seemed unreal that the day had passed so quickly. But the water squishing in my boots was the temperature of Bernard Devoto's classic martini and that peanut butter sandwich had settled to a numbness that matched my toes. We had a long walk ahead in moon shadows, and if I could get her to go home we might make it before midnight.

Clinic

Small streams can be particularly difficult late in summer when water levels are at a low ebb and trout retreat into pockets, undercuts, and what few deep pools may exist, where a close approach will simply spook the fish. Inevitably, you will find yourself casting over almost dry places to reach the wet places in order to stay out of sight. There is a real challenge in this kind of angling, and a 10-inch trout can look like Moby Dick when finning in thin currents. For that matter, on a modern featherlight, 2-weight outfit, so ideal for small streams, a 10-inch fish is a splashy adversary.

The snap pickup, as already mechanically described, is easy to learn, and while there may be only a few occasions to use it in the course of a day, it's good insurance against broken tippets and lost flies. In Eastern limestone streams and on many Western rivers where emergent elodea and cress beds are common you will find the snap pickup a perfect solution to fishing those glassy pockets between weed sweepers; here, snagging is almost inevitable, especially with the nymph, or wet fly.

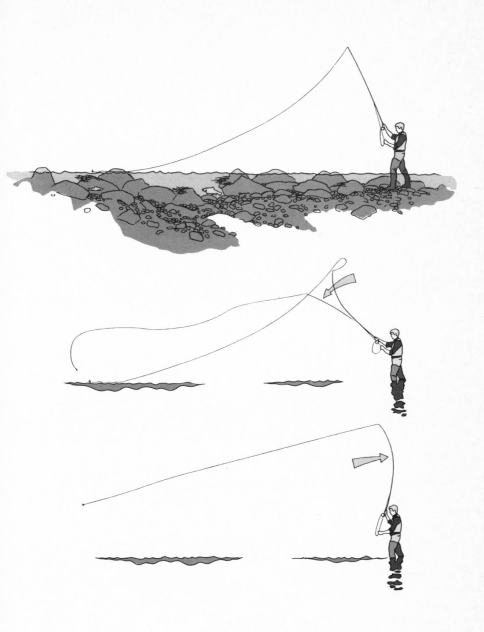

Snap pickup

20

THE PLATFORM OF REGRET

In the geographically circumscribed world of the Atlantic salmon angler, the rivers of Norway represent an Olympian height. Each season fish of 40 to 50 pounds or more are caught in the fjord country, and the world record of 79½ pounds—captured in the Tana River—has remained the standard to beat since 1928.

Such angling is not something one just finds. A beat (which can vary in size from a small pool to a mile or more of river) may be rented; or it is possible to join a syndicate that controls the entire stream; or, if money is no object, one may rent the entire river. There are countless alternatives and none is cheap. On the better rivers in Norway today, such as the Driva, Maals, Reisa, Sand, Alta, and Laerdal, the prices vary from $300 to $1,400 or more a week per angler, for fishing privileges on a beat shared with three to five others. An important rental in Norway or Iceland (which is comparable in price) may go for $120,-000 or more for the season, which is less than two months. The torrent of shillings, francs, and dollars that has poured down the fjords during the last century would stagger the imagination.

It was in this heady atmosphere that I visited a river broker in Bergen who represented the Laerdal River (also referred to as the Tonjum, its old name). This magnificent watercourse has played host to King Michael of Romania, the Prince of Wales, Prince Axel of Denmark, and Prince Wilhelm of Sweden. My broker had the firm, disinterested handshake of a man accustomed to dealing with royalty and doing his daily push-ups.

"You are most fortunate," he said softly. "How would you like King Michael's beat?" I felt a shrinking sensation in my traveler's checks.

"Well, uh, I am looking for something *modest.*" I could hear Patti screaming now. No Copenhagen. No Paris. No Vienna. No wife.

"Ah, but it's uniquely available for the next two weeks. The last tenant died. Quite suddenly." I was tempted to ask how. He shuffled through a small metal file on his desk as if he were viewing French postcards. "Here we are—the Tonjum beat, which includes the Platform of Regret!"

"The what?"

"The famous Platform of Regret, known throughout the world for its big salmons. Ha, everybody regrets having hooked one!" He sat back and laughed. I missed the point.

As I didn't want the Tonjum cottage, the maid, or the cook, but elected to stay at the Lindstrom Hotel, we arrived at an equitable price. The lease gave me two miles of the

Laerdal River, and the services of two guides or *kleppere*.
One guide would have been quite enough, but Olaf and
Oddvar were prerequisite. After I signed the agreement
my broker mentioned that the Horse Pool downstream
from Tonjum was also available.

"It's good insurance to have Horse Pool because it
always holds salmons. And it's cheap."

Drunk with my success I signed for the insurance,
blithely assuming that as a two-*kleppere* man already, I was
adequately staffed. It wasn't until the first morning after we
arrived at the Lindstrom Hotel and were greeted by a
phalanx of guides that I learned about Hans and Peter,
who came with Horse Pool. They treated me with a defer-
ence indicating that I was heir to King Michael's platform
and that Fort Knox was my personal piggy bank. Patti and
I marched out of the lobby with our *kleppere,* who were
carrying their gaffs at right shoulder arms, and we were
met by two cars—each with a uniformed chauffeur. Nobody had mentioned a chauffeur. The chauffeur is subcon-
tracted to the *kleppere* (after all, you've got to get from point
A to point B), so we did the only equitable thing: Patti got
in one car with Hans and Peter and I went with Olaf and
Oddvar.

Just as pine in functional design has become known as
Early American, the well-built Laerdal houses, which reflect industry and thrift, might be called Early Norwegian.
The main street is bisected here and there by forlorn rivulets that come weeping down from the steep mountainside
to seek their parent river.

The Lindstrom Hotel once dominated the village (it
burned down about ten years after my visit). The hotel had
been famous since before the turn of the century. This
imperial playpen had been host to all Europe's crowned
heads bent on catching salmon, and the more successful
anglers were celebrated by wood carvings and painted out-

lines of their prize catches, which adorned the walls of the inn.

The cuisine at the Lindstrom, far removed from the Continental influence of large cities, was what we came to appreciate as "back-country" Norwegian. Every meal began with an amazing variety of herring, largely because fresh herring are readily available. Fjord people are a vigorous race of farmers and fishermen, and thus the food is hearty—the pressed cod, or *persetorsk,* or, for stronger stomachs, the *lutefisk,* a cod prepared in potash lye. Another aged fish dish, and one much appreciated in Norway, is *rakorret,* or raketrout, which is half fermented by storing the fish in a barrel with coarse salt and sugar and pressing them under a heavy weight for three months. Cattle are scarce, and the staple meat is mutton in the form of *fenalar,* a cured smoked leg, or *pinnekjott,* the salted and dried ribs. Game birds come to the table often, and the favorite is *ryper,* or ptarmigan, a delight to all people living along the south rim of the Arctic Circle; venison, or *dyerstek,* is, in Norway, the meat of the reindeer. But salmon, particularly the *rokelaks* in smoked form, has the same prestige and market value in Norway as it does elsewhere in the world.

"Ve first *dr-ry* Horse Pool," said Olaf somewhat uncertainly, as if he wasn't sure whether he had a good idea or not. We drove down an apple-blossom-covered lane and stopped next to a barn to view the river. True to its name, Horse Pool had horses on its banks. But the Laerdal was in flood, and the animals were mucking around in shoulder-deep water which covered an adjacent cauliflower patch. They looked like a school of Loch Ness Monsters rooting in the bottom. We tried to wade across the field wearing chest-high waders, but it was hopeless. Even when conditions are perfect, salmon have a maddening habit of "resting" in certain widely scattered places. There may be only three or four spots in two miles where the fish tarry in their upstream migration. The edge of the unseen cauliflower patch was one such place, and the next was a short stretch of the Laerdal where it parallels a busy highway. The only way the highway portion could be fished was by walking along the guardrail and casting while keeping an eye open for traffic.

"Now I know what happened to the last tenant," Patti growled as she walked behind me. "He was hit by a truck."

I nodded vaguely. The Praetorian guard finally came to a halt, and after a brief conference Olaf announced that we would go to Tonjum and the Platform of Regret.

Platform fishing is unique to Norway. Elsewhere the angler casts from a canoe or boat, from the bank, or by wading. But here many of the large rivers have such a steep

gradient and torrential flow of water that normal methods
of approach are impossible. The empty-bellied squall of
gulls rang clear over the booming of nearby glaciers as I
walked the planks which, though secured to the bank,
curve out over the river and end abruptly at the head of the
Tonjum Pool. The hissing Laerdal tugged at the frail sup-
ports, and the platform swayed underfoot. I looked back
and saw Patti sitting among the boulders with Olaf, Oddvar, Hans, and Peter. Their steel gaffs glinting in the sunlight—and their grim expressions—reminded me of Abbé
Sieyès, who, when asked by the French court what he did
during the Revolution, said, "I survived." It didn't help my
balance at that precise moment to see a pair of great fish
arch over the stream in long thrusts of burnished silver.
Although fish overcome their uneasiness by exuberant
leaping, the angler who trods the Platform of Regret in
high June water has no such recourse.

I began casting at the very end of the walk. Standing
3 feet over a flow that would have torn the *Queen Mary* from
its anchor, I aimed the fly, a gaily dressed Jock Scott fash-
ioned from the feathers of a speckled turkey and florican
bustard, married to strips of red, yellow, and blue goose
with teal, mallard, golden pheasant, with a bright touch of
silver tinsel—a panoply of color that salmon are known to
relish the world over. But not today. A half hour later I
changed to a Green Highlander, then to the old reliable
Blue Charm. But if my unseen audience was bored, my four
kleppere skipped the whole performance. They were asleep.
Patti went off looking for wildflowers. I was convinced that
the two salmon who seemed to applaud my entrance on the
Tonjum platform had continued on their mystical journey . . .

Life for the Laerdal salmon begins and often ends below
the Ulvis waterfall, or *foss,* an impassable cataract on the

uppermost reach of the river, not far from Tonjum. The parent 'fish swim up the 115-mile-long Sogne Fjord, the longest in Norway, which runs like a deep cleft into the barren, purply mountains. Then, entering the Laerdal in June, they pass ten weeks in reaching the *foss*. The eggs are seeded in their gravel beds by huge, scarred fish that have grown dark with winter's first chill. Taxed by their long journey from the ocean, many of the adult spawners die, but others make it back to the sea. In its lifetime, an Atlantic salmon may make two or three spawning migrations; however, fewer than 10 percent ever return to their natal stones. When the golden pearls of spawn are hatched, the young remain in fresh water from two to five years, depending on how fast they grow (it takes three to four years in Norwegian rivers). When they reach the length of 5 to 6 inches, they are called smolts. The smolts make their downstream journey to the sea, and, while many Canadian salmon, for example, return to Maritime rivers after just one winter in the ocean, as grisle weighing 4 pounds or more, Norwegian fish usually remain in the ocean for two to four winters and come back to their rivers weighing from 10 to a possible 60 pounds. Why Nature arranged this distribution of sizes is not known, nor is the sea life of the salmon fully understood. There is positive proof that salmon from both sides of the Atlantic travel thousands of miles to share a common feeding ground off the coast of Greenland: Fish tagged in Norway and Scotland and New Brunswick and even Maine have been recaptured in the Davis Strait where they find an abundance of capelin and sand lance. Undoubtedly, other sub-Arctic areas also attract salmon from both continents.

How a salmon finds its way around countless miles of ocean and unerringly returns to its native river remains a mystery. This phenomenon has been subjected to extensive research, but the homing mechanism does not appear to be a single factor so much as a progression of circumstances.

Perhaps most importantly, it has been learned that a salmon can "smell" its parent stream. Water is not a consistently flavored liquid. There are various substances dissolved in it which come from the soil, the air, and the metabolism of its organisms. The olfactory sense of a salmon is keen. The fish can distinguish organic materials below the odor-sensitivity threshold of man. Strictly speaking, the senses of smell and taste are combined in a fish; water passes through conventional holes in the snout, but instead of connecting with a throat passage as in man, it goes into small sacs that are highly sensitive olfactory organs. While each river has a distinctive "aroma," the individual salmon reacts differently according to its familiarity. Remove the olfactory organs and the fish becomes lost.

This, however, does not explain how shoreward migrations are achieved from the high seas where familiar odors do not exist. Salmon do show a keen awareness of changes in light intensity and length of day—which suggests that the course of a salmon's ocean life is an integrated whole involving the downstream migration of the young, seasonal movements, and exploitation of the environment before a landfall is made.

It was evident from the way my salmon hit the fly that he had no intention of leaving home. One instant my line was drifting in a bow across the river, and in the next it shot straight out into the cauldron of white water as though it had snagged a passing express train.

Although a full-grown man outweighs a full-grown salmon, the shock of a 40-pound, 4-foot-long fish against a 6-ounce rod is electric. Rolling its body and pounding its tail in the heavy current, the salmon has an awesome pull. The game as it is played in Tonjum is to keep the fish in the pool, never letting him run far from the platform or reach the rapids below. Norwegian anglers use heavy, two-handed fly rods with 70- and 80-pound-test leaders, so they can lean back and work their fish hard. But the challenge of angling is to impose a handicap by taking a trophy on the lightest practical gear. My 10-pound-test leader brought a pained expression to the faces of my *kleppere* who, of course, believed in direct action. I prayed that the fish would live up to its ancient Roman name of *salar* by immediately leaping, thus tiring more quickly and discouraging a marathon run. The Platform of Regret was just 100 yards long, and if the fish decided to head straight down the fjord I would have to leave the quaking boards for an even more dubious footing. All I could see out of the corner of my eye was a steep, rocky bank, barbed-wire fences, and trees. Fishermen are notorious for giving advice at critical moments, and for the first fifteen minutes I was admonished by my four acrobats, none of whom I understood. They bounced behind me on the platform shouting. It was like running a relay race on a trampoline. My line sliced through the water, and the reel screamed a banshee wail.

"You're putting too much pressure on him. Loosen the drag," shouted my faithful wife. I wondered how she cut into the snake dance between Olaf and Oddvar. Oddvar, who looked like the late Ben Turpin, practically fell in front of me making a clock-winding motion with his hands to indicate that I should tighten the drag. Peter disagreed with Hans and they got into a singsong argument until the salmon shut everybody up by finally vaulting in the air and coming down in a bellywhopper that sent waves across the Laerdal. My left hand was numb from reeling by the time I got the salmon coming gently into quiet water near the bank. Then it happened. In a great burst of energy, the salmon streaked out into the current and plunged down the fjord. I had to run and run fast. There was no more platform.

My four *kleppere* followed me to the first barbed-wire fence. In the Indian summer of life, one does not charge over an obstacle course willy-nilly; I made a frantic search for a loose strand or broken post, but finally Hans and Olaf pressed their weight on the wire and I straddle-hopped it, tearing my pants. Running like a madman with a 9-foot rod held overhead I went across a field that would make a lunar landscape look like a ballroom. I have known backbreaking work on 500-pound tuna and 1,000-pound marlin, sitting in a fighting chair for an hour or two, keeping the pressure on until my hands turned to jelly and the leather harness squeezed my ribs like an Iron Maiden—but this was ridiculous. The next thirty minutes were a nightmare of dodging around trees, stumbling over rocks, and even losing a shoe which I couldn't stop to retrieve. My lungs heaved like bellows. All I could remember was that Jack MacCormac of *The New York Times* took the deep six doing this very same thing on this very same river. Twice I caught up to the salmon and started him into shallow water again, but there was still some steam left in his engine—and none in mine.

The game finally ended at another barbed-wire fence, only this one went across the river. If the salmon had made one last spurt, he would have been home free, but I nudged him slowly over the stones until his back was out of the water; then he flopped on his side. I dropped my rod, got one bloody hand under a gill cover, and with my other hand got a firm grip on the "wrist" just above his tail and dragged all 45 pounds, 6 ounces onto the gravelbar and flopped next to him. It was the biggest Atlantic salmon I had ever caught, and from my horizontal position he looked like a silver whale. Patti was the first to arrive, still clutching a fistful of violets and buttercups.

"Well, I'll give these to whichever one of you doesn't get up. Who won?"

"Don't be funny," I panted. "Call my broker and tell him . . . tell him Mr. McClane sends his regrets . . . but he has to sell."

Fingering the spool

Clinic

For heavy gamefish I prefer a handcrafted reel with a smooth drag system. However, any fly reel with a good click mechanism is a viable option if you use finger pressure inside the spool to prevent a line overrun, or to get additional drag when needed. Some fly reels are made with a flanged spool that extends over the frame so pressure can be applied on the rotating rim with the palm of your hand. Unfortunately, I never got a chance to insert a finger on my last Laerdal trip with Curt Gowdy and hockey star Dennis Potvin (who is as quick with a rod as he is with a puck). Not only is the old landmark hotel gone, and a tour-busstop motel in its place, but the platform has been washed away in a flood, and the village, now supermarketed and super-highwayed, could be Westchester suburbia. No "forlorn rivulets"—only the sound of a nightly invasion of the motorcycle brigade. Salmon still come to the Laerdal but, as everywhere in Salar's kingdom, not in the numbers or sizes of years past. The once-remote Ulvis waterfall is now also a tour-busstop. So much for progress.

21

GRAYLING WITH GUSTO

Whenever I hear "The Sound of Music," I don't think of all those sun-crazed people jumping around on top of an alp, but rather of the sight of grayling dancing a cappella ballet in the currents of the Traun. When the film was being made, photographer Arie deZanger and I were on a three-story assignment for *Esquire* that took us from Vienna to Geneva by way of Salzburg. The Salzburg stop was, you might say, a dividend, with the Traun River nearby, and who could ignore that in the merry month of May?

There was a greasy fog hanging over the Autobahn on the drive from Vienna, then a splatter of hail that turned to sleet, then snow, then rain. By the time we reached the Bristol Hotel, the thermometer and barometer had bottomed out. Julie Andrews, Christopher Plummer, Eleanor Parker, and for that matter the entire movie crew were sprawled around the lobby, or bellying up to the bar. The only color in that somber scene was Ms. Andrews, who looked smashing even in a soggy mackintosh. Raindrops rolled off that pert nose like living pearls. The weather had been "hosing" over Salzburg for weeks, and if there was an exciting story here, it was probably the producer talking to his banker back in California. In this direction lies madness.

Well, Arie and I got our act together the next morning and took off for the fabled Traun. Our first beat was upriver near Bad Ischl, where they had recently gouged a new highway out of the mountain, sending slides of boulders down an almost vertical slope. We could have used pitons to get to the stream, whose golden bottom was now blemished with tin cans, auto tires, pop bottles, empty crates, and even a dead chicken. I waded out and stepped on an old mattress, promptly getting my boot jammed between some loose springs. Despite all the rain, the glacial Traun has a quick runoff, so the water level wasn't too bad; but under a pewter sky the air was frigid. Arie went stumbling downstream someplace muttering to himself in plumes of icy vapor. His figure disappeared into the haze.

In the meantime, I blindly worked a quarter mile of river before I got away from the roadside and hooked my first Traun grayling. Even in that leaden water, I could see its spectral form rise vertically from the bottom, then take the fly in a rolling dive. I have caught many grayling over the years, and I honestly wouldn't rate them very highly as a gamefish, but for some reason those found in the Traun pack an extra wallop, even leaping from the water in a manner not typical of the species. This one made two arc-

ing jumps and almost made it into my backing. Measured against the rod, it was an 18-inch fish—about average for the Traun. (General Arthur McCrystal, who lived on the river for many years while informally operating his jolly McTraun Casting and Culture Club, recorded one of 27 inches in the dim past, which probably weighed more than 6 pounds.)

Before the day was out, I caught a modest number of brown trout and more grayling, killing a brace of the latter for dinner. Arie had another pair in hand when we met back at the defunct chicken, and together we climbed sloth-like through a cold drizzle up to the highway.

When we returned to the hotel, I delivered our fish to the kitchen. Most of the *Sound of Music* cast was sitting around the lobby watching the paint peel, but Arie and I joined Chris Plummer at the bar. He had the cabin fever syndrome. One of the dancers, a nubile young maid, asked me—inasmuch as I am a sports type—if I could work a charley horse out of her leg. Off the record, I admitted that every card-bearing member of the Outdoor Writers Association of America is an expert in such medical problems, and ultimately I relieved her ailment, much to my surprise. Such was my uncredited contribution to *The Sound of Music*.

Ah, but the dinner brightened our otherwise injured world. They never heard of cholesterol in Austria. We began with a miniature omelet flavored with freshly picked woodland mushrooms in a fine dice of wild onion. This was followed by our grayling, split and boned, then grilled in tarragon-flecked butter and accompanied by an ethereal sauce Choron. This was washed down with a vintage Gewurztraminer, the most fragrant of white wines. After a medallion of venison, redolent of black truffles, we devoured a bowl of chilled raspberries dolloped with crème fraîche. At the time, Arie and I didn't realize that we had to face a week of this debauchery before getting on to our next assignment: the restaurant of Marius Bise in Talloires, perhaps the world's greatest. The only thing that saved us from our massive lack of willpower was the daily cliff scaling and arduous hiking along the Traun.

Charles Ritz opened his classic book, *Pris sur le Vif* (*A Fly Fisher's Life*), with the statement that grayling "taken on the dry fly, must be placed at the head of the salmonids." During the many years we fished together, I found that he could change his mind about casting and tackle technique more often than you and I change our socks, but on grayling he was adamant. To Charlie, trout and salmon were second-class citizens. His reasoning had nothing to do with the game qualities of grayling, but rather emphasized "the effort of concentration, the skill and mastery it demands from the fisherman." To anybody who has defended himself against the suicidal onslaughts of arctic grayling, say in remote Alaska or in the Northwest Territories, this is a pretty strong statement. However, like so many things about angling, there are few rules and many exceptions. In Charlie's world, the slick and gravelly Ain, Doubs, and Loue rivers of France, the Ammer in Bavaria and above all the Traun in Austria developed what is genetically best about grayling. Invaded since the days of Roman legions, these streams hold stocks of fish that would prejudice any nonbeliever. They grow micrometers for eyeballs and with a 5X tippet you might as well pursue them with a frog gig or similar piece of equipment.

The grayling in the Doubs at Lilliaton drove me nuts one day, with their up-and-down refusals (Charlie called them elevator inspectors), until I resorted to Ben Hardesty's infamous 8X. Then, with my usually heavy hand, I broke off more fish than I care to remember. It was, of course, typical of Charlie to be in his glory when angling became a technical nightmare. Nothing could satisfy him until persistence paid off, as it often does. On that worst of days, he landed a handsome 2-pound, 9-ounce grayling. Using the rule of thumb that any "trophy" fish is half its particular record, M'sieur Ritz made the problem look as easy as a game with baby blocks on the floor.

Grayling do not grow to a large size; fish of near 5 pounds are in the record category for Canada and Alaska. The largest known for Montana was a 2-pound, 10-ounce grayling taken from Handkerchief Lake in 1974. Until 1978, I had never taken a grayling from the Madison River that measured more than 10 inches. During recent seasons, however, an encouraging number of 14- to 16-inch fish (estimated at 1¼ to 1½ pounds) have come to the fly, which may be an indirect result of Montana's fairly recent and successful wild-trout management policy. The American grayling, *Thymallus arcticus,* has a life span of about 12 years in arctic waters, and 10 years in the southern part of its range, though here most fish live less than 6 years. The European grayling, *Thymallus thymallus,* grows somewhat bigger, with a record 7 pounds, 7 ounces from Rostojaure, Sweden. It has been rumored to attain 8 pounds or more in Lapland, but in several long junkets through those mosquito barrens I've never bettered 2½ pounds. In Yugoslavia, which has many grayling rivers, the sport is quantitative. On the chalkstreams of Britain, where grayling abound in the Test, Itchen, Kennet, and Avon, a fish of 4 pounds is virtually a museum specimen; the record there is 4 pounds, 9 ounces, and was taken in 1883.

Grayling cannot be described as having a typical body color or color pattern. There are five recognized species in the world, and various populations run the gamut from pale silvery brown to purple in some Alaskan rivers, and even to black in one Eurasian species. What makes the otherwise homely, puckermouthed fish unique and beautiful is the pink- or lavender-spotted saillike dorsal fin. The male's dorsal is larger than the female's, and while it may seem an extravagance of nature, the fact is that during reproduction the male positions himself next to the female and, leaning toward her, folds his dorsal over her back to be perfectly oriented during that brief second when eggs and milt are expelled.

In comparison to trout, grayling produce very little milt and only a modest number of ova (from 1,000 to more than 13,000 eggs in a large fish). Furthermore, some populations do not have an annual breeding cycle. In fact, the spawning of individual grayling may occur at two- to three-year intervals. So the sex act is critical and the fin a conjugal blessing to a species with limited reproductive capacity. To look formidable, the male will erect his dorsal when discouraging the amorous advances of other bucks at the spawning site, or when repelling egg thieves such as ravenous brown trout (an endeavor in which the grayling meets with very little success).

Another unique anatomical feature of the grayling, much less apparent than its dorsal, is that its eyes have pear-shaped pupils. The pupil is round on the side farthest from the snout, but tapers to a point on the side opposite. Whether or not this accounts for the grayling's curious behavior when rising to a fly is purely speculative. Unlike a trout, which holds its feeding station high in the water and rises to insects forward and laterally, the grayling lies deep, rises almost perpendicularly, then plunges back to bottom. The take may occur 3 or even 10 feet to the rear of the grayling's holding position, depending on the depth of the water and the mood of the fish, but it will rarely be forward or in a lateral direction from the feeding lane.

Specialized eyes always have a function, as in the case of the adipose eye of the bonefish, but the pear-shaped pupil is an enigma. Perhaps it is a legacy from the thymallids' origin in the Eocene period, 70 million years ago, when torrential rivers and arctic darkness demanded visual skills that are no longer essential to survival. Obviously any fish that can nail a #22 dry fly in swift currents by rising from 8 or 10 feet below the surface has keen eyesight. Even when they were coming fast to the mayfly minutiae of the Doubs, my fly color and size had to be exact. They were faithful risers, studying every one of my patterns before diving for gravel. I wasn't sure if they were laughing at me or trying to help me select the proper imitation.

Our last day on the Traun was the first good day the movie company had on location. The sun burst over Salzkammergut and the lobby was pure bedlam when Arie and I went down to breakfast. You could sense the emotion, the feeling of being the only survivors in the world. They were even rehearsing in the hallway, hootin' and hollerin' and jumpin' like starved trout after stoneflies.

Thanks to a dinner invitation earlier in the week, our angling drill was going to be at Gmunden. Arie and I had been invited to the Berndorf castle of Archduke Franz Josef. The chowdown was a formal, candlelit affair, and deZanger, the greatest scrounger since Ghengis Kahn, borrowed threadbare tuxedos and boiled shirts for us from two of the hotel's waiters. We looked like a pair of soup-stained penguins. But despite our eccentric appearance among the ancien régime, the evening produced offers of beats at Marienbruke, Steyerberg, and Gmunden.

Even with the run of these three classic beats, we still took a daily shot at the cliff near Bad Ischl. It was the "hot spot" for big fish, according to local sages, but today the only news here was that our dead chicken had floated away downstream.

After we checked in with the river keeper at Gmunden, he walked us down through a meadow riotously colored with buttercups and purple cyclamens to a stretch of water that reminded me of the old Beaverkill. It could have passed for that once-great pool above the bridge at Cooks Falls, where the current splits at the top with the main flow angling away over a deep ledge before it accelerates into a bouldery run down below. The morning sun illuminated the water, and by standing among bank willows we could see the dark forms of grayling slowly rising and settling over brightly polished stones. Oscar Hammerstein was correct in his lyrics—the hills *were* alive with the sound of music, echoing in a hundred swollen springs gurgling from that pristine meadow. I eyeballed one big grayling poised near the ledge; but at hip depth, I had to cast at nearly a

90-degree angle. The fly swept in a wide arc out of the fish's feeding lane. This proved to be the bugbear of that idyllic beat: trying to get "lined up" on individual fish. We hooked a good number of grayling, however, by casting upstream and down with long slack floats. It wasn't like the halcyon days of Great Bear Lake or Alaska's Ugashik, but who counts without purpose? I managed to take one 22-inch fish on a #22 fly with my little Perfectionist, which in itself made the day memorable.

Reluctantly we hit the road for Geneva late that afternoon, and made it over the French border to Talloires by the following morning. Geez, we were six days late. Arie and I figured that fishing with the rained-out movie company was a dangerous excuse to offer that grand maître de cuisine Marius Bise (all famous chefs are temperamental— you better believe it). After doing 300 restaurants, I could write a book about kitchen karate.

As things turned out, this jovial Gallic Santa Claus was not only forgiving, but he owned the best trout and grayling stream in Haute Savoie. And food? Well, we were made welcome with a velvety pâté of woodcock marinated in brandy, followed by a dish of dilled crayfish, then trout done in the blue style, followed by roasted wild hare with chestnuts and wild currants. We saluted the hare for its noble demise with a vintage Château Ausone, my favorite red wine for a game dinner. Overall, it was one of the most delicious meals I ever had. These notes are gravy-stained, tear-stained, or smeared with fly-line flotant. I can't quite remember which.

Somewhere the Good Book says, "Thou knowest not what a day may bring forth."

I'll buy that.

Clinic

The peculiar rise form of a grayling is completely different from that of a trout. Grayling do not hold in a near-surface position when feeding on top but come all the way from the bottom, more or less aquaplaning backward with the current, and drifting downstream in the process. Once the fly is taken the fish returns to the bottom and repeats its rise, as if going up and down in an elevator. In deep, clear pools

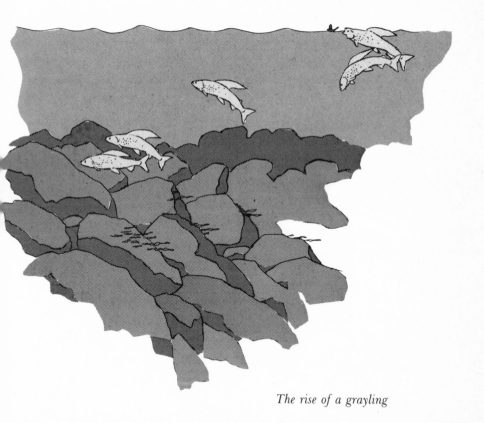

The rise of a grayling

it makes fascinating angling, seeing the fish on its upward drift before the strike.

European grayling are largely insectivorous but our American species is more omnivorous, particularly in the arctic and subarctic, where a variety of small fishes and isopods such as sow bugs and scuds are dominant food items. I find the most effective dry fly in northern waters is a #12 Black Gnat, or Black Ant, and for sunk flies any of the sow bug or freshwater shrimp imitations in gray, dark brown, or black dressings. For streamer flies to imitate minnows or leeches, patterns such as the Muddler Minnow or Black Wooly Bugger are especially effective in areas where large grayling are common.

22

SOMETIMES THERE'S A SALMON

Atlantic-salmon fishing is the ultimate roll of the dice. I've won big, broke even, and crapped out as often as the law of averages permits. Aside from the collywobbles that frequently possess Salar's soul, there are droughts and floods and other unpredictable phenomena that have left me fishless, or nearly so, on the best salmon rivers in the world. For a nonfeeding fish to gobble a fly called Hairy Mary or Rusty Rat, conditions must be absolutely right. And I am never certain what the right ones are, as my best days—for instance, a day of snow with gale-force winds in Iceland—often look like disasters to me. (Even the sea gulls flew backward on that day in Iceland.)

Despite all this, a salmon river is an innocent force of nature, a companion in our leisure hours, and I've never met one I didn't like—whether it was flowing darkly through the spruce-crowned valley of the Moisie or trickling among the lily-bordered runs of Ecum Secum. Those magic places—Three Islands Pool, Serpentine, Malangsfossen, Deva Coapoacho Pool, Helens Falls—have a quality of otherworldliness where placid silences are broken by the sounds of splashing salmon. Maybe it's because Aquarius is my birth sign, but I'm content just to stand in a river watching parr attend the sunset dance of the caddis—a promise of continuity in an age when obsolescence of material things is built in—seemingly into civilization itself.

In 1981, 1,202 Atlantic salmon were caught in the eight public rivers in Maine, and, with various restoration programs under way throughout New England, there is some hope that more Americans will know the joys of chasing this noble gamefish before the end of the next decade. In 1986, when the last fish ladder is in place in Wilder, Vermont, it is expected that salmon fishing will exist in the 407-mile length of the Connecticut River. There is no question that the angling will never be what it once was—a game played in lonely places with only a vagrant moose for an audience— even if the Connecticut, Merrimack, Penobscot, and Saint Croix run pure and silver again. These streams will be utilized to their fullest. Despite the fact that there are some 400 salmon rivers in eastern Canada, and more and more being liberalized or opened to public fishing in Quebec, which began disbanding private-club waters in the 1970s, the popularity of *Salmo salar* only spirals with availability. Almost 90,000 anglers pursue the Atlantic salmon in Maine and Canada today.

Salmon fishing in North America differs from that in Europe in a variety of ways. With a few exceptions in Quebec, Canadian rivers as well as those in Maine are restricted to fly fishing only. Another distinction, an optional one, is the tackle used. Among European anglers the double-handed fly rod in excess of 12 feet in length is by far the most popular tool. Shorter, single-handed rods of 8½ to 9½ feet are dominant here, however, and even lightweight 7½- to 8-foot graphite and boron rods are effectively fished in low water. If there is a standard for rivers of the western Atlantic, it would appear to be a 9-foot rod calibrated for an 8- or 9-weight line. And as a bonus, the salmon come readily to a dry fly in many rivers—even in the subarctic latitudes of Labrador. The theories advanced for their reluctance to surface-rise in European streams are legion, but it does add an exciting dimension to our fishing.

Salmon are not seeking food when they enter a river. The fish roll or leap over the surface occasionally, probably because of energy built up from long months of feeding at sea. They are not rising to insects, so the traditional concepts of fly fishing have no value. There is no viable hatch to match, and it may take an hour or more to get a fish interested in a fly.

On rare days they will strike almost recklessly. One June morning on the Sutter of the Miramichi, four of us had almost instant hookups with 20- to 28-pound salmon. We each had to make a mile run on foot down a long riffle because the fish were too strong to hold in Home Pool. Carl Tillmanns started the marathon, Peter Verstappen ran behind Carl, Bill Briggs followed, and then I came along, hooked into a bright 26-pounder that made 11 beautiful jumps. After hiking back to the pool, we all hooked salmon again—not as quickly this time, however, which was just as well, as my second trip through the shallows and over slippery boulders was as graceful as a drunk staggering off a bar stool. On the very next day we had to pound the water to a froth to get even one fish.

The salmon season begins in high, spring water when big, showy 2/0 and 3/0 wet flies are fished with sinking or sinking-tip lines. After the runoff and clearing currents in June (or July in the Far North), the effective fly sizes diminish; when water temperatures reach 48° to 50° F, you can switch to a floating line and use smaller #2 to #6 flies that swim closer to the surface. As the river level drops and warms into the 60s, even smaller wet flies from #8 to #12 and floating patterns down to #16 will tempt more and more fish. Essentially, this is a game of repetitive casting until a fly of a given size and shape, worked at just the right depth and speed, is accepted. This may even seem to be strictly a matter of luck, but it has a stylized ritual. You can shuffle through the box, try a fat Muddler, a slinky Blue-and-Silver Tube, Green Butt, Buck Bug, Midnight, Cosseboom, Surface Stone, a golf-ball-size White Wulff, even a perfectly tied Jock Scott with all twenty-four exotic ingredients in place, then finally coax the fish up to a #14 Brown Skater. The idea is to present different silhouettes, deep or shallow, floating high or low or skimming the surface. Like some whimsical Nero, a big salmon may spend two or three weeks in a pool, critically reviewing the flies of 100 anglers before rising to a solid take. Even on days when they are coming to a "hot" pattern, repetitive casting to a visible fish—or at least a known lie—is the basic tenet.

Rating the Atlantic salmon as a gamefish is difficult, simply because most of us are lucky if we can afford one or maybe two trips per season. Over a period of thirty-five years I have dunked my waders in every salmon country from Spain to Labrador for a total of about 100 weeks, which would amount to possibly 450 to 500 fish. My best catch was a 45-pound, 6-ounce salmon in Norway. Despite its impressive size, the fish did nothing more than a surface roll, then ran stubbornly downriver for more than an hour. Fortunately we were fishing the deep-flowing, log-filled river from a boat and were able to follow the salmon in the boat as it covered over two miles. It wasn't a spectacular bout, but it kept my adrenaline pumping.

I can count my lifetime allotment of big salmon on one hand, but it's my impression that the middleweights in the 18- to 28-pound class are the real scrappers, and Canadian salmon more so than European fish. Although we caught a number of 20- to 30-pound fish on that Norway trip, only a few made any attempt to justify their species name, *salar*, "the leaper." Yet these were all bright June migrants at their peak of condition. I've had similar experiences in various European streams and am convinced that the most acrobatic fish are found in the Maritime Provinces. My most memorable fish was a 22-pound Miramichi salmon taken on a dry fly in low summer water that made sixteen furious jumps—a classic contest on a light graphite rod.

An Olympian beat in Iceland or Norway can't be had cheap. Today it would run from $3,000 to $5,000 or more

a week. But this is no guarantee of great salmon fishing, or even that there will be any taking fish in the river. On the other hand, many Canadian outfitters offer package trips (mostly fly-in) at modest costs, where with any luck you may limit out every day. There's also good angling available on a daily fee basis, especially in New Brunswick and Quebec. Public salmon fishing that requires nothing more than a license has a carnival atmosphere—the participants queue up and shuffle down a pool in rotation—yet it produces sport for thousands of fly casters. Although there have been rare instances of ill temper when some joker decides to become a permanent fixture at the top of a lie —and there was one act of senseless terrorism in 1982, at Cherryfield, when a marauding band of hoodlums ripped up the public facilities on the Narraguagus—the future generally looks bright. Nowhere is this more evident than on the public streams in Maine, where neophytes and veterans now crowd the rivers.

One morning I watched a skinny, fuzzy-cheeked boy playing a salmon on the Machias. For twenty minutes he stood rooted in one spot, clinging to the rod like a caterpillar to a violently shaking limb. The fish did nothing but circle the pool. A large audience ringed the lad and offered encouragement, but the salmon gradually edged to the deep far side that was full of downed timber. The play came to a stop. Two men shouted "Hang on, kid," and ran over the boulders and back to the parking lot. In minutes they returned, puffing under the weight of a cartop boat. They slid down the bank, scraping their shins, and one man lost a shoe. By the time they launched the boat our angler was almost in tears. The men worked skillfully, following his fly line with a paddle edge and lifting it free with their hands. The one-shoed character submerged his arm in a mat of smelly algae and nearly went overboard. With pained expressions they finally raised a sodden tree limb with the fly attached.

There are those who argue that quality angling will never survive without the elitism (and therefore economic responsibility) synonymous with expensive private clubs, or the limited access offered by outfitters at premium prices. Lord knows I've had a costly career in that respect, but in these changing times the salmon and its habitat are being mercilessly destroyed by every instrument from nets to acid rain. The image of the elitist—popular in the days when gentlemen were said to throw salutatory brandy snifters into the fireplace—is of course as false as the egalitarian concept is true. Responsibility for any fishery is a painful process of education. It wasn't too long ago that a no-kill stretch on a public trout stream was regarded as heresy, yet the majority of anglers are in harmonious accord today.

Considering that the total catch on the Penobscot in 1981 came to 800 fish (out of a tallied 3,500 in the river), one would expect that the killing of salmon is accepted practice. The happy fact is that some anglers have been releasing fish; and indeed, the local Veazie Club has started promoting a self-imposed limit of 5 fish per year as opposed to the 10 that are legally allowed. This could set a precedent for the future of public angling—if it survives the commercial onslaught. It is a complete break with tradition. In most of Europe, where the money value of a river increases with the number of fish killed, thus establishing higher rental charges for the future, a dead salmon is fundamental to the sporting concept. This is not to be taken lightly by any visitor with a reforming urge, either. Release a salmon in Norway and your continued presence will be as welcome as the bubonic plague. Unfortunately the salmon has a very high price on his head.

Izaak Walton called the Atlantic salmon a "king" among fish, and he would turn over in his crypt at the sight of a burly gray-haired woman standing in a shallow tributary of the Penobscot, lustily beating a salmon over the head with an aluminum camp chair—an ironic coronation after a crusade of 2,500 miles from its winter palace off the coast of Greenland. Oscar Wilde would have called it the "nasty dimension of truth," yet the blatant poaching that has spread like a virus is as old as the greed of humankind.

Today five different governments pursue their own salmon interests with drift gill nets on the high seas, where the world's genetically different stocks are totally mixed and therefore impossible to manage. The crown, I think, is on the wrong head. It reminds me of the *Festum Asinorum,* that medieval Feast of Fools, where the ruling powers of the day were personified in a parade of crowned and robed jackasses. The logical answer lies in the "headland principle" of treating each river as an ecological entity, with salmon harvested in the estuaries of their home streams where the checks and balances of population dynamics can be evaluated.

I don't know what tomorrow will bring, but I'll be back at Home Pool with my feet in gravel starting blocks, hoping that I can still run that mile. It gets tougher every year. But if nothing else I can wait for the parr to dimple; they will be fewer in number, so I'll say, "Hang on, kid, the good guys are coming," and wonder about its truth.

Clinic

There are days when the first fly you tie on the leader will take salmon, especially when you are fishing with a guide

De Feo Skater

Salmon Skater

Pink Lady

Dark Hendrickson

Hair-Winged Rat-
Faced McDougall

White Wulff

Muddler (Spuddler)

Rat-Faced McDougall

Cosseboom

Jock Scott

Birds' Stonefly
(nymph #2)

Hunt's Wasp

Birds' Stonefly
(dry)

Salmon-fly design

who is already aware of the taking patterns from yester-
day's trip. However, a hot number can suddenly turn off,
and there is always the individual fish who is immune to an
otherwise provocative Buck Bug or Cosseboom. Fly fishing
for Atlantic salmon often evolves into a fly-changing routine, repetitively casting patterns of different sizes and silhouettes with success depending on your persistence. One
trick worth trying is the riffled fly; this can be done with any
wet pattern already knotted on the leader simply by making
a half-hitch in the tippet and tightening it behind the eye
of the hook so the leader now extends from the *side* of the
eye rather than directly from it. The hitch should be
secured on the right side of the fly if the current is flowing
from right to left (facing across stream), or on the left side
of the fly if the flow is left to right. This will cause the fly
to skim on the surface as it swings in its arc, a movement
that often triggers strikes when orthodox presentations
fail. Keep enough tension in the line for a smooth swim—
or slack off if it starts to motorboat and throw a wake.

23

THE BAITCASTER'S BARRACUDA

Gil Drake, proprietor of the bonefish paradise otherwise known as Deep Water Cay, flipped a surface plug across the bow of a motionless barracuda. Tapping the reel handle and whipping the rod, Drake doodled the lure in erratic, rolling hops over the crystal-clear water. For a moment we could see the fish slowly turning, as though listening to the plug still some 20 feet away; then with the speed of a serpent the cuda flashed through the shallows and sped across the flat. The act of hitting the lure occurred so fast that only the loud swish of monofilament and the tortured hoop of the rod revealed a strike. About 50 yards out the barracuda made a long, vaulting, open-mouthed jump that covered at least 10 feet horizontally. Without pause the fish jumped again, rotating in the air this time, then barreled off in a semicircle.

Fifteen minutes later Gil boated and released an estimated 20-pounder. Shortly after that he was hooked into another one. For fast plugging action, barracuda in shallow water are hard to be beat. Tied tail-to-tail with a pike, or muskellunge, which the barracuda resembles, old razormouth would turn either one inside out.

For all his faults and talents, the great barracuda (*Sphyraena barracuda*), from his broad tail to his pointed head, is a first-class gamefish. Of some twenty species of Sphyraenidae found in the tropical and subtropical seas of the world, the one called "great" is really a plug buster. The only area where he doesn't occur is the eastern Pacific. Here a smaller, less spectacular relative consorts with the party-boat trade. It is believed that the great barracuda reaches 6 feet in length and attains a weight of about 100 pounds. The present record listed by the International Game Fish Association is an 83-pound fish from Lagos, Nigeria. However, any fish in the western Atlantic over 40 pounds is exceptional, and the average is probably closer to 10 pounds. But there is no denying that all barracuda *look* big when they sneak up behind a plug.

In 1963 I was asked by the State Department to accompany King Mohammed Zahir of Afghanistan, who was then visiting the United States, on a Gulf Stream junket. His Royal Highness had sailfish in mind, but since it was the wrong time of the year for spindlebills we had to settle for something else. Our outing happened to be during one of those rare periods when the blue water is absolutely dead, and after hours of fruitless trolling I asked the king if he would like to catch a barracuda. Coming from a landlocked country, the king didn't have a clear notion of what we were after, but he agreed. We roostertailed north to a wreck buoy marking one of the freighters that went down to a Nazi sub during the 1940s, just two miles from Jupiter Inlet. No sooner had we put our baits out when the barracuda appeared—not big, but hungry. The king was enthralled that a fish could be located with a buoy and caught so readily. I explained that barracuda, like good politicians, know when to open their mouths, which may be more fact than simile.

The majority of great barracuda are caught by fishermen who are trolling offshore for some other species with comparatively heavy tackle. This is seldom interesting, as the fish usually sounds and rarely displays his aerial ability. Although barracuda have been taken on live bait at depths greater than 200 feet, they are most frequently encountered on reefs, flats, and along mangrove shores. These shallow habitats are not wholly the territory of small barracuda; in many regions, notably the Bahamas, fish of 10 pounds or more may consistently be found in knee-deep water. There is obviously some migration to the open sea due to temperature changes, with the largest fish coming on the flats with the first cool weather in the fall.

Normally, in the Cave Cay area for example, large cuda appear directly against the bank on a rising tide. As a rule, the flood and high water are the best fishing periods; as the water falls the cuda retreat to nearby channels. Around small Bahamian islands—which are often divided into two types of habitat, with marl and turtle-grass flats on one side and steeper coral shores on the other—you can predictably locate the fish according to the stage of the tide. To some extent this is also true in the Florida Keys, but elsewhere along the coast the occurrence of big barracuda inshore is spotty. The reason may be simply the lack of suitable habitat or the greater variation in water temperature to the north.

Barracuda eat other fish, and their dietary preferences

reflect what is available in a particular location. In the Bahamas, for example, we often see them feeding on needlefish, which are common along the mangrove shores. In Florida, cuda pursue the more abundant mullet. However, everything from the almost sedentary puffers to the swift-moving mackerel are consumed. From an angling standpoint this would seemingly allow a wide choice of lures, but for all practical purposes the selection is rather limited.

Barracuda are eminently a plug caster's specialty. They can be caught on long, slender bucktails and popping bugs, but fly fishing is hard work. As a rule, you need to make very long casts, and the fly must be retrieved at a speed that is faster than most people can strip line. A hundred curious barracuda will follow a fly for every one that actually strikes. This makes it a tedious game. Once, while doing a TV film on barracuda, I caught several over-20-pound fish on the fly at Thrift Harbour in two days of the toughest kind of casting I can remember. Small barracuda may strike readily to slow retrieves and short casts, but an old razormouth demands action in his baits and you can dislocate a shoulder before hanging the first big fish with a fly. Personally, I enjoy the faster pace of baitcasting with light tackle, particularly in view of the fact that barracuda are suckers for top-water plugs and tube lures. Some of the wildest strikes I have ever seen were made by 10- and 12-pound barracuda, with as many as a half dozen fish rushing at the same plug.

But don't think that baitcasting is an easy game. The way we fish for barracuda in the Bahamas is to stalk them along mangrove shores by slow-poling parallel to the islands. Although the fish are big, it's surprising how many you can spook in the course of a day. Unlike bonefish, which are almost constantly moving about, barracuda lie motionless and may appear as nothing more than shadow on the bottom. During high tide they often lie right up among the mangrove roots, and because of their ability to blend into any background even a 4-footer is hard to see until you've had some experience. Small sharks, such as the lemon, shovelnose, nurse, and blacktip, are always common in the same areas, but these can easily be distinguished by the undulating movement of their tails. The angler, of course, stands in the bow and watches for targets.

When sight-fishing on the flats I never cast near a barracuda. A lure that splashes close will invariably send the fish flashing off to deep water. Too close, by my definition, is within 10 feet of a visible target. There may be the exceptional cuda that will strike reflexively at anything that falls within reach, but such fish occur at the ratio of about 1 out of 100. It is far more effective to place your lure 10, even 20 feet ahead of or beyond the cuda and bring the bait across his line of sight.

When a barracuda wants to hit a plug or tube it's impossible to reel fast enough to get it away from him, so the technique is to draw the fish to the lure rather than to cast the lure to the fish. This should be accomplished at the greatest practical range; short casts are not as effective as medium to long ones of 60 to 100 feet. Most big cuda stalk a bait for some distance, and with a short cast you'll quickly bring the fish into view of the boat. Although the cuda has an overpowering curiosity and will examine a skiff like a prospective buyer, 9 out of 10 of them lose their appetites the instant an angler or hull is visible. At times, they can be as spooky as double-domed Battenkill brown trout, even when densely schooled.

Speed of retrieve is the key in triggering strikes. It must be rapid and erratic. If the lure is retrieved slowly, one or more barracuda will follow the bait but make no attempt to hit it. If the lure is stopped, the barracuda will stop and quickly lose interest. If the lure is worked at a fast pace, and the barracuda pursues it without striking, a slight *increase* in its speed will generally bring a flashing hit. As a rule, this is not hard to do because the reaction of the individual barracuda is obvious.

It has long been believed that barracuda are attracted to flashing objects, and that spoons are ideal lures. I have not found this to be true. Spoons have some value in deep-water trolling, but I have experienced too many occasions when a wobbler wouldn't attract fish at all, and for casting in shallow water these subsurface baits are impossible to operate because they constantly hang in coral and grass. I took a 5-foot, 5-inch, 44½-pound cuda back in 1951 at Walker Cay on a little ⅜-ounce plunker, but the lure hasn't been productive since. For some reason, plugs under 4 inches in length don't excite big cudas with any regularity. The most effective lure is a 12- to 15-inch length of surgical tubing or "tube lure" that can be skittered on the surface or worked underwater.

One of the most common questions asked about barracuda is: Will they attack man? The answer is a very qualified yes. Attacks have been authenticated by the unmistakable wound (like a cleaver slash) in the victim; in a few cases the fish has even left his teeth in the flesh for positive identification. I am well aware of the fact that spear fishermen skewer numerous barracuda every year, and that skin divers often swim around them with impunity; nevertheless there are many records of both provoked and unprovoked attacks. There's no point in elaborating on the gory details here, as they have been well documented by Breder, Gudger, Coppleson, Hutton, Randall, and other scientists. Statistically, a swimmer splashing at the surface in turbid water—not a wading angler—is the most likely victim. At all times, large barracuda should be treated with respect—in the water or aboard ship. I once watched a guide swing a billy club at a barracuda, and at the critical instant the fish kicked free and the guide hit his sport squarely between the eyes. It took me a week to recover.

One of the zaniest barracuda trips I ever made was back in 1959, when things were getting hot in the Congo. I met an old *colon* by the name of Albert Fisher who owned a 40-foot diesel that traded on the west African coast. The morning we left the dock at Banana Point, Fisher handed me a Portuguese flag. The Belgian flag was already flying topside.

"When I signal with my hand"—he made an upward punching motion—"you will be obliged to raise the Portuguese flag."

"Why?" I asked.

"They may shoot at us from Bulabemba across the river." I didn't ask any more questions because Fisher already had the boat under way. I changed flags six times before we got out of the river mouth—always under the steely stare of cannon.

Four miles offshore the echo sounder showed a ridge from 200 to 1,000 fathoms. Two Baluba tribesmen whom Fisher had hired as strikers, and who were now very seasick, set out a pair of flat lines (with the reels upside down) and put a pair of feathers in our wake. The lures hadn't dropped back 30 feet when they were both hung into barracuda. Now, this African species (*Sphyraena jello*) is different from our great barracuda, averaging close to 6 feet in length and bearing arrowlike brassy green markings along the flanks. They are heavy and strong. Exactly what happened when the fish struck is a little vague, but if you've ever seen a pair of crotch-clothed Baluba climbing a gin pole with a pair of angry barracuda snapping at their heels you'll know what I mean.

Neither neo-angler bothered to crank the fish in; they merely dropped their respective rods and took the cuda hand over hand. The fish arrived simultaneously at the transom, and, taking the wire leaders, the boys both swung their fish aboard. It was like watching an accident in slow motion. Few cockpits can accommodate a total of 12 feet of surprised, very much alive barracuda. You wouldn't have seen such dancing at the old Peppermint Lounge. Fisher finally coaxed his boys down from the gin pole after one cuda had sunk his teeth in everything, including the footrest of the fighting chair, where he impaled himself, and the other had finally slid down the open engine hatch. We ate the barracuda that night, after the old man assured me that fish poisoning was unknown in the Gulf of Guinea —but at that point anything wacky seemed perfectly normal.

Great barracuda are eaten in many tropical areas, but the flesh of those over 3 pounds in size is so often poisonous that it's not worth the risk to cook one, and certainly not in the western Atlantic. The poisoning (ciguatera) is due to a toxin in the flesh and not from bacterial action or decay. Evidently, the toxin originates with a microscopic dinoflagellate that grows in the algae formed on the exposed surfaces of broken coral. Herbivorous fishes or "grazers" feed on the algae, and thus the toxin enters the food chain. The Pacific barracuda (*Sphyraena argentea*) is an exception. This fish has never been known to be poisonous —it is, in fact, one of the more popular food fishes in California.

You will hear many tales in the Caribbean about how a poisonous barracuda is identified—by its size, the color of its teeth, the rigidity of its scales, the presence of a milky secretion on the body, and the fact that the flesh will turn a silver coin black—but it's all bunkum. It's like playing Russian roulette. However, dubious edibility in no way detracts from its sporting qualities. Some of the finest saltwater gamesters—such as the bonefish, tarpon, and permit

—have little, if any, value as food. Unless the fish is to be kept as a trophy, the barracuda should be released like any other noble champion.

Of course, there are countless places in the world where one can find good barracuda fishing, and there are plenty of hot spots throughout the Bahamas. Two worth noting, however, are the Cross Cay area, about 12 miles north of Deep Water Cay, and those flats between Jacob's Key and Red Shank to the south. This is still virgin territory, and around a long chain of small cays we found not only an abundance of barracuda but bonefish and permit as well—a "no lose" parlay by any angling measure.

Clinic

There's no question in my mind that the tube lure is the most reliable bait for barracuda. The slender tube evidently resembles a needlefish undulating over the surface —a prey that barracuda can't resist. Assuming that you have cast the lure beyond the fish, get the tube moving at top speed. The barracuda will chase it from long distances, closing the gap so quickly that often the strike will come within a few seconds after the retrieve commences. However, the object is to get the fish to hit before it sees the boat, so if the barracuda hesitates and stalks the tube, stop the retrieve and pump the rod two or three times to keep the lure "alive," then start reeling again. If a big barracuda doesn't take on the first cast the odds against your success with second and third casts increase greatly.

For the fly fisherman there is now a Cuda pattern streamer, a 9- to 10-inch-long imitation of the needlefish made of a material called Fishair; like the tube lure it has a lifelike wiggle in the water. The Cuda fly can be worked at a slower pace than orthodox bucktail or hackle-feather-wing streamers, and, because of its inherent action, trigger strikes while you are stripping line at a comfortable speed.

One of the many idiosyncrasies of the great barracuda is that the juveniles tolerate warmer water than the adults and the big ones move onto the flats during cool weather. The best period to look for trophy fish inshore is during the winter or early spring season.

24

BIRTHDAY BLUES

While I was reading Hal Lyman's book *Successful Bluefishing* the other night, a number of unrelated events came to mind that will add nothing to his exhaustive treatise on *Pomatomus saltatrix,* which is the most complete study to date. As every reader of his chaste publication, *SaltWater Sportsman,* already knows, its former publisher stared into a crystal gluepot periodically to predict the eccentric migrations of a fish that is obviously mad as a hatter and not amenable to summary. Ray Bergman could write a book called *Trout* and be reasonably certain that his subject would be swimming in the same stream tomorrow, doing the proper things that trout are expected to do, and with-

out fear of having his subject bite him. Commander Lyman has no such advantage, yet he walks the literary plank with uncommon skill.

My first recollection of bluefishing goes back to 1928 when Governor Alfred E. Smith of New York was running for president against Herbert Hoover. The governor went fishing for snappers at Hampton Bays. That is to say, he made some vicious slaps at the water with a bamboo pole as though exorcising Shinnecock Canal. This demonstration was for the benefit of the press as Smith had no credentials as a sportsman. I happened to be sitting on the dock (hardly a day passed when I *wasn't* sitting on that dock, only a mile from my grandfather's house) and, never having seen a head of state—least of all a potbellied, cigar-smoking dandy in a tailored suit with polished shoes peeking from under a pair of spats, wearing a brown derby while fishing—it boggled my six-year-old mind.

His angling technique, however, was recalled many years later by a postcard that Charles Ritz sent to me when Dwight D. Eisenhower was running for president. An uncompromising expert, Ritz had taught the general how to fly-cast, an art form that obviously requires some manual dexterity. The maestro reported, "I believe he will make a good president but unfortunately he doesn't know how to use his left hand." In any event, Governor Smith finally kicked his bait can off the dock, seemingly by accident, and the Fourth Estate repaired to a famous watering hole known as Canoe Place Inn. He lost my vote on footwork alone. All the gunk in his bait can splashed on his spats.

Juvenile bluefish or "snapper" were one of those ubiquitous species, along with cunner, porgy, and blowfish, that filled the void in many American stomachs during the Great Depression that began a year later. They could be collected around any coastal pier, or for that matter in the Hudson and East rivers in the summer months. You'd see people shouldering soggy burlap bags of fish on the trolley cars and subway trains in Manhattan, and the Long Island Railroad began its weekly "Fisherman's Special" to Montauk, which was always jammed to the doors. Some 30,000 people bought tickets every season. Although called "snapper" because their razor-sharp teeth click like castanets, those little fish bear no relation to the true snapper family. A baby bluefish (under a pound in size) is soon known by another euphemism, "chopper," which describes its lusty adult existence.

In his *First Report to the United States Fish Commission,* in 1874, Professor Spencer F. Baird drew a portrait of the fish which does not exaggerate its character:

The Bluefish has well been likened to an animated chopping machine, the business of which is to cut to pieces and otherwise destroy as many fish as possible in a given space of time. Going in large schools in pursuit of fish not much inferior to themselves in size, they move along like a pack of hungry wolves, destroying everything before them. Their trail is marked by fragments of fish and by the stain of blood in the sea, as, where the fish is too large to be swallowed entire, the hinder portion will be bitten off and the anterior part allowed to float away or sink. It is even maintained, with great earnestness, that such is the gluttony of the fish, that when the stomach becomes full the contents are disgorged and then again filled. It is certain that it kills more fish than it requires for its own support.

The feeding frenzy of bluefish is a phenomenon that has no parallel in the marine world. Even sharks must be stimulated by some unnatural condition such as the presence of a chum slick or quantities of fish caught in a net before they will blindly pursue their prey en masse. An extract from the *Gloucester Telegraph* on June 4, 1870, describes what must have been a mother lode of blues during a period of cyclic abundance:

Accounts from New Jersey say that the Bluefish came in at Barnegat Inlet last week, sweeping through the bay, over flats as well as through the channel, driving millions of bushels of bunkers before them and filling the coves, creeks, ditches, and ponds in the meadows full. At Little Egg Harbor Inlet they drove shad on shore so that people gathered them up by wagonloads. Fish lie in creeks, ponds, etc., along the meadows 2 feet deep, so that one can take a common fork and pitch them into a boat or throw them on the bank. In some places they lie in windrows on the meadows where the tide has taken them, so they take large woodscows alongside and load them.

Although there had never been a recorded instance of bluefish attacking people until April 11, 1974, the chances of such a vendetta occurring again are good. What the press failed to note was that eleven bathers were bitten at Haulover Beach in Miami, Florida, on that Thursday, and that while the news was in print that Friday, the choppers attacked again, biting at least five more people. When I say "bite" I mean that one victim, a fourteen-year-old girl, required fifty-five stitches to close her wound. The blues were apparently in the 10- to 14-pound class, as about 100 of this size were caught at a nearby pier. What makes the second incident so alarming is not only the occurrence of the first, at a time when the water was literally churning with big fish feeding on pilchards, but the fact that on the very next day, with the same frenzied activity in evidence, people blithely went swimming again among the marauding schools. This is about as safe as jumping into a bathtub full of piranha.

It almost seems ludicrous that so savage a fish could be the subject of a romantic idyll, but John J. Brown comments in *The American Angler's Guide* (1849) that bluefishing is a mode of piscatorial amusement for the inhabitants of Connecticut, New York, and Long Island.

It is usually performed in a good-sized sail-boat, with a guide who knows the ground, or by casting from shore, and drawing in alternately. The former method is most practiced, and being highly approved of by the fair sex, who often compose the best part of the fishing party, of course stamp it at once with perfection. To those ladies who unfortunately have to be placed on the list of invalids, and can endure the delightful and bracing summer breeze

and gentle south wind, a few days' sport in the Sound,
with a bluefishing party, will amply repay their exertion.

Robert Barnwell Roosevelt in his *Gamefish of the North-*
ern States of America (1862) was particularly fond of Fire
Island Inlet and described how on a summer day one could
see the white sails of fifty boats tossing about in the roll of
the breakers. He advised the reader to land on Raccoon
Beach at noon "and either cook his fish by a fire built from
the wraiths of the sea, or get a fashionable dinner from
Dominy or t'other man that keeps a hotel there." He further suggested that the bluefish be accompanied by cold
champagne. I must admit, champagne would not be my
choice as a mate to the oil-rich fillet of a bluefish (I'd prefer
a robust red wine), but then Congressman Roosevelt published his book under the pseudonym "Barnwell" and nobody could fault him for bizarre tastes.

The dynamics of bluefish populations are not understood. It's wildly possible (my own theory) that Nature
long ago imposed some balancing gene in its most predaceous marine organism to compensate for any overactivity
such as the almost lemminglike population of 1870. According to Zaccheus Macy in his *Account of Nantucket,*
bluefish were very abundant around the island from the
time of the first settlement by the English in 1659, and
were taken in immense numbers from June until mid-September. The fish disappeared, however, in 1764, and
didn't arrive en masse again until 1800. Dr. Samuel L.
Mitchell stated that bluefish were entirely unknown around
New York prior to 1810, but that they began to be taken
in small quantities along the wharves in 1817 and became
abundant in 1825. Huge schools appeared off the coast of
New Jersey in 1841. Throughout the history of this fishery,
highs and lows occur in a totally unpredictable pattern.
Since 1970 the catch by sport fishermen alone has ex-

ceeded 100 million pounds annually from Cape Cod to Cape Hatteras, but this could collapse tomorrow.

The bluefish is a species common off our Atlantic Coast from Florida to Cape Cod and in warm years north to Nova Scotia. Within this range they migrate from south to north in our spring and summer, and from north to south in the fall and winter months. Evidently spawning occurs mainly in northern waters as the young summer fish or "snappers" are only known in the area from Chesapeake Bay to New England. So the season for bluefish is variable, beginning in December in Florida and finishing by April, and beginning in May and ending in October in New York waters. In his book, Hal Lyman covers the various racial stocks and their migrations to the extent that any hard information is available.

There is one thing about the blues off Florida in April, however, that I have never seen described, and that in fact we only observed for the first time during the 1960s. The jumbos—fish in the 18- to 20-pound class, which are rarely caught inshore—appear in their northern migration 6 to 10 miles out in the Gulf Stream. Charterboat skippers trolling for sailfish have been cleaned out of baits in short order by these huge schools. Whether the jumbos are traveling by way of Cuba or simply represent the terminal-size population of our Florida fish is pure speculation. There are normally fewer boats offshore at this time of the year—and certainly no small-craft bluefish specialists (since our Southern fishery, unlike the north, is almost wholly an inshore operation in bays, inlets, and the surf, but seldom more than a mile or two outside). It's possible that a major portion of our runs is untapped.

Bluefish inhabit other parts of the world: along the entire east coast of South America, where they are known as *anchoa,* and from the Azores to Portugal, where they are called *anchova,* and south to the Cape of Good Hope in

Africa, where they are known as *elf*. Migrations also appear
in Mediterranean North Africa and the Black Sea where
they are variously called *pesce serra, strijelks skakusa, gofari,*
and *lufer*. They are also common around Australia. I have
never fished for blues outside of the United States, simply
because it is the kind of fishing I can do at home. However,
I did witness a run, probably comparable to the one reported by the *Gloucester Telegraph,* at Isla de Margarita off
the coast of Venezuela. Back in 1957, when George Bass
and I were doing some exploratory marlin fishing out of
Porlamar, we headed for the barn late one afternoon and,
entering the channel, we saw natives running along the
beach in all directions, toting gunnysacks. The sand was
covered with pilchards, the pilchards were covered with
flopping bluefish, and every few seconds the water would
explode, sending another shower of prey and predator
ashore. It was an awesome sight. The water below us was
black with southbound schools, evidently headed for Bra-
zil.

Bluefish are caught by virtually every method from
surf casting to fly casting, and Lyman's book goes into
considerable detail, obviously drawn from long experience. One of the peculiar traits of bluefish is that, despite
their periodic feeding rampages when you can't avoid
hooking them, there are glut periods when the fish are
present but almost passive in their response to baits or
lures. During one of our big local runs in years past, this
usually started out with blues pouring through the inlet to
Lake Worth, savaging the mullet schools and snapping at
every bait in sight. For the next two days fishing would be
so easy that after a few hours you had enough fish in the
boat for the whole neighborhood. I could lose a dozen
bucktails or popping bugs in no time at all. But this would
be followed by a slack period.

Although bluefish appear every season in Florida waters, we seldom have one of those bonanza migrations. One *big* run occurred in 1963, and the day was January 26. It was my birthday. I've never been fond of "surprise" parties, but my wife conjured one up, the gimmick being to have my pal Ed Reddy keep me out fishing all day. It wouldn't have been such a *long* day if the fishing was poor, but we were on the Lake Worth flats by 8:00 A.M., and at 5:00 P.M., after catching more bluefish than anybody could count, Ed was saying, "just one more." I thought Reddy was going bonkers. We were casting top-water baits blind and sometimes to visible feeders but it didn't matter. Fish were everywhere, mostly in the 6- to 10-pound class, and they put on aerial displays I'll never forget. The bars we fished varied from 3 to 5 feet in depth through the tides, and blues are real performers when they can't sound. But after nine hours of sheer bedlam I wanted to go home. We kept only about ten fish but we looked like victims of a tong war—bluefish blood, Reddy blood, and McClane blood all mixed. Bluefish are not easy to release. Anyhow, when we finally walked in the front door, me lugging the stringer of fish, about seventy people shouted "surprise." I nearly had a coronary.

If one fishes for bluefish, inevitably one eats bluefish, and this is a somewhat neglected subject. At best it's very good, soft-textured, of long flake, and mild-tasting in small sizes. Although there is no hard evidence to back me up, I think our southern bluefish in Florida are of better flavor than northern stocks. We know bluefish have a catholic appetite and will consume literally any species available, but the most abundant forage in any region is their obvious first choice. In Southern waters bluefish feed chiefly on mullet, pilchard, and anchovies, whereas the very oily and strongly flavored menhaden or "mossbunker" becomes a chief item of bluefish diet as the schools progress north. During peak years in the bunker cycle, blues gain an off taste. Young "snappers," on the other hand, are always sweetly flavored, as they feed on crustaceans, mollusks, and various small inshore fishes, notably the silverside, which gourmets know as "whitebait."

As in all highly predaceous fish, the digestive enzymes of the bluefish are extremely powerful and the meat will spoil within a few hours of being caught if left ungutted without ice. A bluefish must be dressed as soon as possible after taken from the water. Since the meat has a high oil content, it does not travel well unless icing is continued. For the same reason be sparing in the use of oils or fat in creative recipes; the best recipes contain neutralizing acids in the form of fruits such as lemon or lime. In common with other swift-moving pelagic species such as the tuna or mackerel, bluefish have a large amount of muscle hemo-globin in the form of a dark strip of meat which can be removed from the fillet. Although extremely nutritious, it's perhaps too "fishy," even slightly bitter, to some palates when served hot; yet it's delicious when cold.

Small "snapper" blues are ideally pan-fried. Fresh from the water, gutted and scaled, they have a delicate flavor. In common with many other species, however, the larger this fish grows, the less flexible it becomes in the kitchen. Blues up to 6 or 8 pounds are the perfect size for baking and broiling in fillet form. Fillets of large fish (over 10 pounds) can be carefully trimmed, to remove all the dark meat, and made into chowder. Perhaps the best method for very large whole fish is to bake them over charcoal in a covered cooker, then chill and skin them to serve cold with a sour-cream-and-lemon dressing the next day. This is a marvelous way to prepare blues in the 15- to 20-pound class—if you should be so lucky. In any event, reading Hal Lyman's book is bound to improve your chances of sampling this noble fare.

Clinic

Gone are the days of our great bluefish runs in Lake Worth, when the inlet and waterway were carpeted "wall to wall" with hundreds of skiffs as anglers joyously boated big choppermouths. Today, the bluefish schools mostly bypass the Palm Beach inlet and head in a more southerly direction. As a result, my occasional trips for this species in recent years have been to Montauk and around Martha's Vineyard and Nantucket. The most interesting fishing has been in that tidal sweep of Cape Pogue Gut at Chappaquiddick Island. I fished there recently with charter boatman and light-tackle specialist Captain Bruce Parker out of Edgartown. Playing jumping bluefish on the fly in the swift and shallow gut is akin to hooking Atlantic salmon in a thundering Norwegian river. A 9-foot fly rod calibered for a 10-weight-forward line proved to be ideal; although wire leader tippets are usually recommended, we used 12 inches of 60-pound-test hard monofilament in front of the fly without a breakoff.

Edgartown, incidentally, is home base for the annual Genesis Fund Fishing Tournament, which deserves some praise. The tournament was created in 1982 by basketball's great John Havlicek and Edward "Spider" Andresen, now publisher of *SaltWater Sportsman*; all the monies raised in this contest to see who can catch the biggest and the most bluefish and striped bass are donated to the Birth Defects Institute. It would be a great leap forward if more fishing tournaments were designed to fund such worthy charities. In this case, everybody wins.

25

BASS BUGS AND ORANGE JUICE

Abner Coots and I were sitting years ago under a loblolly pine on the banks of the big Satilla in Georgia just before dawn. We could hear the soft snapping of duck wings as the birds went over before the light, and Abner allowed as how the way to hunt or fish is for as long as you live and not be caught running out of time or trying to do something in less time than you really have. And I wondered as he talked if that was why he was such a good fisherman.

We had taken bass after bass from Kinchatoonee and Muckalee creeks and in the limestone sinks around Albany. After we left the red hills, we went down to the backwater to fish the Ogeechee and Canoochee, and Abner all the while had that slow yet vindictive rod stroke of a man who could cast one way for one fish until the rivers ran dry. As we paddled down the big Satilla that morning, he talked his bass up to a strip-skin bug as if he didn't particularly care how it all came out. "Just come up and see the bug," he seemed to say. They came, slow in starting, but when they took hold, you could still hear them afterward echoing in the tupelo gum.

While driving on to Dale Hollow, Tennessee, the next day, I tried to remember all the big bass I'd caught with bugs, and I arrived at the magnificent total of *one.* Maybe two. And I recalled two that got away. My arbitrary "big" would then have been a largemouth of 8 pounds or better and a smallmouth of 6 pounds or more.

In the interest of precision, it is not amiss to observe that very few large bass are caught with bugs. Big bass are caught on plugs and plastic baits, with live bait running a poor second. By way of example, I can point out that of 443 prize-winning bass (to 1954) in the old *Field & Stream* contest, 263 fell to plugs, 101 to live bait, and 63 to spoons or wigglers. A remote 16 succumbed to flies and bugs. It might further be observed from these statistics that bug fishing is hardly worth writing about. But among my readers there must be a few who are not horrified by these revelations, and who will sacrifice their other methods that pay so well for a richness of angling enjoyment.

I'd never go fly-rodding for bass with the idea in mind that I would catch a big fish. This game consists of nine parts fun to one part bass. To exceed the ratio in favor of the fish is to lose a basic angling concept. You would groan to read of the heavy but careless bass with whom I've made passing connection entirely unredeemed by Waltonian nourishment. Abner and I agreed that it is best to work for something you want over a long period of time and learn about it thoroughly, because sooner or later you will be good at it, and your luck will change.

Bass bugs are designed to imitate frogs, mice, moths, and other large forms that fish find on the surface. While some of them don't look like anything in particular, they at least suggest food to a bass. There are two main kinds of bug: a soft-bodied one made from some animal hair, and the hard-bodied type made from a solid floating material such as cedar, cork, or plastic. Abner's strip-skin bugs, for instance, are made from the fleshed strips of deerskin, which he soaks in brine for toughening and then wraps around the hook shank. These primitive bugs were made by his father at Lake Istokpoga in Florida, and his father learned them from his grandfather. As far as Abner knew, all the Coots family before him had made strip-skin bugs, which seems to give some credence to the belief that southern Indians, probably the Seminoles, were bugging for bass centuries ago. The deerhair isn't trimmed to shape, but merely sticks out in all directions, and in the days before fly rods Abner's granddaddy slapped this bug on the water with a cane pole and called it "spat" fishing.

Bugs with bodies made of cedar are known to have existed in Florida before the Civil War, and the ones southern casters traditionally use are similar to E. H. Peckinpaugh's Night Bug, which originated in Tennessee back in 1906. Peck made his out of cork, a material which came into use on the Missouri and Arkansas spreads of the Saint Francis and Little rivers. Native swampers built them from bottle corks and turkey feathers. But the cork-bodied bug was first sold commercially by John J. Hildebrandt in 1913, and Peckinpaugh, the Tennessee stone mason, devoted all his time to supplying this firm. Then there was Will Dilg and B. F. Wilder, who designed and tied famous Callmac Bugs. When the two men combined names they sold

Wilder Dilg Bugs, which were put out commercially by James Heddon.

Now there are literally thousands of patterns on the market, and some of them are worthless, but you'll have no trouble getting good, workable bugs from your local tackle dealer. Black bass are found in the lower forty-eight states, and most tackle people are thoroughly familiar with the effective patterns for each locality. A good assortment to start with should include the Deer Frog and Popper Frog in the fashion devised by Joe Messinger, a Devil Mouse designed by Tuttle or Austin, or one of Tuttle's Devil Bugs; for the winged hair bug I'd certainly include some like those made by Helen Shaw, such as the Rost Zebray, or Austin's Winged Whisker Bug. Among the hard-bodied bugs you should have at least one feather minnow, like the old Peckinpaughs or Wilder Dilg Spooks, and several popping bugs. Ever since E. H. Peckinpaugh manufactured the first popper back in 1934, there have been hundreds of them put on the market.

One of the reasons I'm so careful about the bass bugs I buy is that many of them don't cast well. I've used at least a dozen different hair frog bugs, for instance, and the only one that ever turned in a good performance on the water was the Messinger Frog. The frog, which was originated by Joe Messinger of Morgantown, West Virginia, back in 1925, is one hair bug that does cast easily, and the popping version of this bait is an old reliable among pond casters everywhere, It doesn't shoot as easily as a dry fly—the bulk precludes that—but it does cast much better than its appearance would suggest, and its feel on the fly rod is much the same as a large bivisible. There is a nice balance between its weight and bulk. The weight of the #4 hook is offset by the air resistance of the body, so that the objectionable "hit" at the end of the backcast is eliminated; conversely, the weight of the hook is just sufficient to over-

come the air resistance of the body and facilitate casting.

The failure to show real fly-rod results on the national scoreboard is partly due, in my opinion, to the general scarcity of casting talent. We fail to use the principles that have survived in angling by trading them for magic lures, lines, and rods. Or we put mystery into the situation when it's not there. Actually, most bug casters I've watched have no line control to begin with, and they lose confidence in what they are doing. There is a great need for a sound knowledge of casting fundamentals in bugging, because the bug is a difficult fly-rod lure to throw, especially on windy days.

To cast the bass bug properly you must often separate your casting planes. If you move your rod back and forth in exactly the same path, your line and leader are likely to wrap around the rod. No matter how well a man casts, a bass bug is highly air resistant, and the unbalanced shape of most bugs causes them to waver when the line loop is unrolling. The backcast should be made with your rod tipped off vertical; a semi-side cast would be correct. This is achieved by bending your wrist slightly as you make the pickup; then, just as the line is nearly extended to the rear, start the forward cast with your wrist coming back to an upright position, bringing rod and line through a true vertical plane. The false casts should be made easily until the proper length is extended for the shoot; on the final delivery, shoot the line very high, releasing it when the rod is in the 10-o'clock position.

This final cast should be made with emphasis, giving the rod a strong push as it approaches the vertical. The high, lobbing pitch will pull plenty of shooting line and lose its momentum before hitting the water. Remember, when you start a cast, pick the line off the water by using two consecutive left-hand pulls, one to shorten the line and the other to tighten it, before false-casting. Otherwise you will be lifting too much line from the water, forcing you to pull the rod back too far. As a result it will be impossible to get enough speed to hold the line high up.

A bugging rod, like any other rod, is the tool that magnifies your wrist speed and nothing more. So it must have a slow, powerful action, bending all the way down to the grip. The fly line is heavier than usual, and the highly wind-resistant bug travels back and forth slowly. You can't force the casts, even if you have a wrist like a blacksmith's, because the rod will soon have a weight which isn't really there. The rod, therefore, "waits" until the line loop is properly executed before it takes a casting bend at the forward drive. A long rod makes a smooth pickup and gives a good high backcast. A stiff, fast rod is ill suited to casting the bug, as the motion of the rod has ceased long before the backcast has straightened out.

Unlike the situation when you are casting trout flies, with bass bugs you have to allow a longer time before you make the forward shoot. As a beginner, it's a good idea to try short distances first; look in back of you instead of in front, observing just how long the lure requires to make its backward flight. With the forward cast, start slowly, an instant before the line straightens out, and accelerate the movement of the rod gradually as you complete the cast.

If the bug has been fished, work it back so that only a few feet of line remain on the surface before picking up for the next cast. If you try to pick up too much line, you'll pull the bug underwater and make a lot of unnecessary disturbance.

I learned one important lesson years ago, when I was drifting with Hoke Wheeler on Fisheating Creek, where it runs into Okeechobee. We weren't having especially good luck with the bass because we couldn't keep the crappie, or "speckled perch," as they are known in Florida, from slapping at every cast. The speckles were about the size of dinner plates and Hoke was having himself a ball. But once in a while we'd come to a blowdown where the cypress limbs promised a bigmouth, and Hoke, who has a face the same texture as an old leather bag, would get that bland expression of a con man making his spiel.

I first met him at a north Florida animal farm, where he made his pitch with free orange juice for Yankee tourists. Hoke would hang around the crowd until their thirsts were slaked, and then he'd tell them authoritatively, but gently, to follow him. Before they knew it, they had followed Hoke through a ticket booth at a buck forty a head. "Give a man something for nothing and he gets mixed up," Hoke observed. "Bass are the same way. That little old bug settin' there is for free, and if you don't hurry a bass you can sell him anything, including the oarlocks."

Working a small section of shoreline thoroughly with

slow, deliberate movements will always produce a better showing than covering a lot of water fast. When making the cast, allow the bug to remain quiet on the water for at least a minute. Jerk or pop the bug, and then move it several feet toward the boat. Try to vary this method of retrieve in as many ways as possible until you find one that will bring up the fish.

Sometimes the fish will hit the bug as soon as it lands on the water; other times the fish will follow the lure for a long time. Sometimes they strike at the lure just as you lift it out of the water and are about to make another cast. Both Hoke and Abner observed, however, that when a man is getting strikes at the boat, he's fishing too fast, and that when the bass bunts a bug with his mouth closed, it's the wrong size, which was then a new one on me. But I recall that when trout make a closed-mouth strike they can often be taken with a smaller-size fly. So there may be something to that.

Bugging in a river is essentially different from bug-casting a lake. The river usually presents more problems. When wading, the average cast is longer and must be accurate. Your own foot and rod movements must be kept to a minimum, and the retrieve must be handled the same way as when you are trout fishing. Of course, the ideal is to cast over feeding fish, but when this isn't possible, you'll have to search probable locations—around ledges, bushes, bank grass, and behind boulders. Sometimes you'll have to make several casts to the same location before a bass will rise.

Once, on the Pee Dee River in South Carolina, I ran into a situation where the bass wouldn't move until they had six or eight servings of the same bug. It happens that way on occasion. In the jungles of the upper river, however, I could tab a bass almost immediately by bouncing the bug off the cypress trees.

Smart operators never neglect the chance to pop their casts against some streamside object; they usually hit their lures against the side of a rock or log in preference to the water, so that the bug descends in an "accidental" manner. Lily pads are commonly used as targets, particularly when the bug is an imitation frog; the counterfeit is plopped onto a pad and, after the disturbance settles, twitched off into the water.

Bugging this way is tough on hooks. The barb needs frequent examination and occasional sharpening. You'll get hung up once in a while, but usually the percentage of bad casts is so small that the size and number of fish taken more than compensate for the additional effort.

It is not good to have a time limit in which you must get your big bass, or possibly not get one, or even see one. But that's the way bugging is mostly, a slow-paced game where you'll have as much fun as any man can expect of angling. The people who are skilled in it have achieved a small, dry wisdom in knowing that their luck will change.

Clinic

Since writing "Bass Bugs and Orange Juice" I did manage to take a Florida largemouth of close to 10 pounds on a bass bug, and my angling pal Frank Valgenti took one that exceeded that mark by 2 ounces. However, that represents

a great many years of fly-rodding for both of us, and my opinion hasn't changed. Plastic-worm and spinner-bait artists are today's winners in quantity and quality, yet there is a special thrill in bringing a bass up to a bug.

For "light" bugging with #4 to #10 poppers, which is typical for smallmouths, I favor an 8-foot graphite rod of 2½ ounces with a 7-weight line. This is viable for bass of any species in many Northern waters. At home in Florida, where bigger #4 to #2/0 bugs are plied in weedy water, I prefer a rod with more authority. Here, I use a 9-foot graphite of 3⅛ ounces and a 9-weight line. Our Okeechobee largemouths often jump, then bury themselves in grass, and it takes strong tackle to get untangled.

As to bug patterns, these come in and out of fashion; the Messinger Frog isn't made anymore, but similar lures are cataloged by other companies. My favorite bug today is a Queen Bee popper with a keel hook version for the weedy places.

26

CHAINED LIGHTNING

The little hair mouse bobbed near the bank while I waited for the ripples to disappear. Just as I raised my rod to begin the retrieve there was a swirl on the surface and a pickerel came out of the parrot-weed jungle in his quick, purposeful way. He stopped a few inches from the mouse in that tense, tail-dropping posture that marks his kind. I couldn't help admiring his malevolent eye and elegant shape, for the greenish-bronze body, camouflaged in black chains, is at once piratical yet beautiful.

The pickerel flicked his pectorals when I twitched the bait, but he didn't move a muscle until the mouse swam off. I teased it along in fits and starts for several yards. Then, with a surface-bulging rush, old chainsides pounced on the mouse. He struck and whirled back to the parrot weed, my line zipping along behind. As the rod became unyielding the fish zoomed upward and leaped. It was a splashy play, no less determined than the acrobatics of the few bass I had caught that morning.

The pickerel turned out to be as long as my tackle box, which by wilderness standards is nothing to brag about. But when you can catch 20 inches of *anything* within 50 miles of a large Eastern city it becomes a significant game-fish. Not only does old chainsides offer the urbanite a chance to hook something big, but he survives under the worst biological conditions.

The world of the chain pickerel extends from Maine to eastern Texas and as far north as the Great Lakes. Geographically, the chain pickerel is sometimes confused with the walleye, because the latter (an entirely unrelated species) is erroneously called "pickerel" in Canada and the border area. However, some very large chain pickerel or *brochet maille* have been caught in Quebec. Chainsides is also mistaken for the northern pike, because both have the same body conformation. Pickerel, however, are quite distinct as gamefish, not only in size but in spirit. For all his bulk, the northern has a porcelain chin, and, pound for pound, the chain pickerel is the more dynamic of the two. Old chainsides invariably jumps when hooked, and a fish of 3 or 4 pounds puts up a real fuss on light tackle.

I was fishing with General Walter Bedell Smith one afternoon on a New York lake when he caught a 29-inch, 6½-pound pickerel; it took him twenty minutes to bring it to net. A pickerel of that size is uncommon, but unlike many gamefish the pickerel gains strength with age. Bedell's fish fought in the water, in the air, and in the boat. Although properly dispatched, it reflexively snapped its jaws when we dumped it into the kitchen sink late that night. The pickerel wound up hanging between two 14-pound bass in the Smith trophy room.

Any chain pickerel over 6 pounds may be called a lunker. I have caught many up to 3 pounds, but only two that passed the 6-pound marker. The big ones are invariably battle-scarred veterans with a long career of lure chasing. On the average, pickerel of 20 inches are five- or six-year-olds; the heavier specimens, exceeding 20 inches, are usually from six to eight years old. A gamefish can learn a great deal about his anglers in that many seasons.

I greatly admire the chain pickerel, though some anglers of my acquaintance have nothing but contempt for him. They complain that he eats other fish, which is true. But so do black bass, trout, walleyes, and all other gamefish worthy of the name. In a balanced habitat, *Esox niger* is less of a migraine than, for example, the prolific but slow-growing yellow perch.

Many people seem unaware that chainsides grow comparatively fast and are easy to catch. And being late-spring spawners, they provide sport right through the winter months. Ice fishermen take them on minnow baits, and on productive lakes the shanty set finds plenty of action, because old chainsides doesn't lose his appetite when the snow flies. But even if the lakes don't freeze, or until they do, you can enjoy wonderful fishing during the cold, gray days of early winter. Using streamer flies and spinners, I have caught literally thousands of pickerel in ice-bordered ponds and creeks. There's no reason for an Eastern angler to put his tackle away just because the bass and trout seasons have closed.

Besides other fish, pickerel eat crayfish, insects, frogs, mice, newts, and just about every living creature that invades their sanctuary, including other pickerel. One might get the impression that pickerel never cease eating, but the fact is they have periods of fasting, as many a disappointed angler has discovered. At times old chainsides will rest quietly in the weeds while schools of minnows swim by his nose with impunity. After his fast he may choke to death trying to ingest a fish as big as himself.

The pickerel's lackluster reputation is attributable to the use of rugbeater rods and multi-gang-hook plugs heavy enough to dismantle a tarpon. The proper baitcasting tackle for pickerel is a 5½- or 6-foot rod designed for ¾- to ¼-ounce lures, and mounted with a small, fast reel and light line. Skish or tournament accuracy tools are perfect. The light-gear principle applies to spin-casting or enclosed-spool reels, which differ in their mechanics but are equally capable of delivering midget baits.

From a sporting angle, lure size is important. Big baits are out. Chainsides has the unfortunate habit of swallowing a lure right up to the swivel. Naturally you get a listless struggle when six or nine barbs lock his jaws shut. But when taken on a single-hook fly-rod lure or a small spinning bait, he becomes a formidable foe. Perhaps the pickerel feels that a little lure has less chance of escape, because, oddly enough, you are less likely to rupture his plumbing with a small spoon than with a large one. Quite often a tiny wobbler will lip-hook him, and at worst it's easy to remove the lure with a disgorger.

Hairline tackle—which means any of the 4- to 5½-foot ultralight spinning rods and a small reel spooled with 2-pound-test line—is ideal for pickerel fishing. Currently I am using a hollow-glass 5½-foot, 1⅞-ounce rod that's designed for lures weighing up to ¼ ounce; actually, it's just on the heavy side of ultralight.

I do not use a wire leader with the wispy nylon. My terminal rig consists of two 10-inch strands of heavier monofilament: a strand of 4-pound-test blood-knotted to the end of the line, and a length of 6-pound-test joined to the 4. An appropriate swivel is clinched to the end of the

6-pound strand. This shock line prevents wear and breakage. However, the 2-pound-test line permits long casts with tiny lures and makes the capture of even a modest pickerel a sporting proposition. When you've hooked a strong pickerel with hairline equipment, the tricky part of the play occurs after you've led him away from the weeds and snags and are ready to net him. Chainsides puts up a terrific fuss at the sight of the meshes or your hand. When you think the fish is played out, he will invariably thresh the water to a boil as you draw him close. With a light line you must play him to a standstill; otherwise you will lose one after another. At all times keep a reasonable length of line between yourself and the fish. Pump him very gently until his energies are sapped. Naturally, you will have your antireverse in the "on" position, and the drag brake set low, since the elasticity of hairline is almost nothing when a fish has been led within reach.

In Florida the chain pickerel, or "jack," has the same long growing season as the black bass, and consequently runs somewhat heavier than in the North. I've fished waters where 2 pounds is the average size, and that is about twice the norm for Yankee pickerel. I have heard many stories of 12-pounders being taken back in the boondocks. I saw one fish over 8 pounds that was caught by a canepoler at Lake Istokpoga.

My favorite method of pickerel fishing is with the fly rod, and almost any minnowlike pattern is effective. My standards are the red-and-white bucktail with silver body, the Mickey Finn, the Yellow Marabou, and the White Marabou. I use #4 dressings, but it will pay you to try larger and smaller sizes too. Streamers may be combined with a 2/0, 3/0, or 4/0 spinner for added flash, but I don't care much for that kind of hardware when I'm fly-casting. Spinners belong to spinning rods.

The hair nature lures, such as bucktail frogs and mice,

are real killers early and late in the day. Pickerel love field mice, and frogs are staple items. Some mouse and frog imitations are heavy enough to be used interchangeably between the fly rod and the hairline spinning outfit. Some days streamers and regular bass bugs move few fish, whereas a little black mouse fills the stringer.

Large dry flies also work well at times. Although one doesn't usually associate pickerel with floaters, I have had excellent fishing when big hatches of dragonflies brought the fish up. However, the good days of top-water action are not nearly as numerous as those on which old chainsides will grab a spoon. The wobbling spoon (particularly a red-and-white pattern), with or without pork rind, is the most reliable pickerel lure. But on the right kind of late-summer or fall day, when you can wade the shoreline and work your fly carefully in each weed-bed hole, plenty of action can be stirred up. Decide where chainsides is lying in ambush and pass the fly in front of him. This is an art. Many casters who are unfamiliar with the species wade where they should be fishing and vice versa.

The pickerel's habitat overlaps that of the large-mouth bass. Ordinarily you will find him around lily pads, or in beds of muskgrass, pondweed, or parrot's feather. Weeds are important to his method of feeding. Unlike the bass, he doesn't often roam about unless food is scarce; the pickerel invariably waits for his meal to swim by. So cover plenty of water in searching for a lunker. Also remember that if you miss a good fish he'll probably be hiding in the same spot tomorrow, next week, or possibly a month from now.

Where the marginal areas of a pond are free of heavy vegetation, the pickerel will face shoreward from the nearest weed bed. If the shallows are choked with grass, he will assume the opposite position, facing deep water. Nature designed chainsides for inshore foraging, and even a lunker will wait motionless in a foot or two of water for a target. Generally, the best fishing area extends from the shore to a depth of about 10 feet. During the summer months, or in periods of drought when the shore areas of a lake shrink from the bank covers, pickerel may move out to depths of 12 or 15 feet, where forage is more abundant. Under normal conditions, however, they stay as close to the banks as possible.

Two other productive locations are the shallow necks between ponds and backwater sloughs. In rivers, pickerel inhabit all grassy slow-water sections and display the same tendency to hole up on a suitable weed bed or brush pile. Again, pay particular attention to backwaters leading off the main stream. More lunkers are caught in these quiet, out-of-the-way places than in the obvious river covers.

There are two points about pickerel technique worth stressing. You can generally get more strikes by casting parallel to the weed or lily beds. The fish hide just inside the grass, keeping an eye on open water. With the lure passing the length of the bed, more than one pickerel will be tempted to strike. Also, large fish are not so likely to follow a bait drawn away from their weed sanctuary across open water. When fishing from a bank, I prefer to work close to the bank, casting parallel to it, rather than to stand offshore and cast toward it. Much depends, of course, on the contour of the weed bed.

The other thing to remember is that, unlike bass, which are tempted by retrieves that are slow to medium in speed, pickerel are susceptible to a moderately fast retrieve. You notice this if you get many follow-ups or close strikes right under your rod tip. Accomplished casters quickly crank out the last few yards of a retrieve, and a pickerel that has been following the lure is often excited into hitting it just as the angler lifts it from the water. If you see fish stalking the lure without striking, reel in faster.

With the standard wobbling spoon, the correct pace is a fast flutter.

On the other hand, surface lures are often taken when perfectly motionless. In fact, floating baits seem to work best on days when there's little activity; a hair frog popped within easy reach isn't likely to be spurned even if chainsides has a full stomach. But—and it's an important but—top-water baits are not always effective when fished slowly. I think much depends on what the lure looks like; an orthodox popping plug might be completely ignored because it doesn't suggest anything our gourmand understands.

The success of spoon-skittering is largely due to the speed and the disturbance created by a lure that is drawn rapidly across the surface. Move it slowly and you get nothing but follow-ups. With the old cane pole, a big spinner or a pork chunk was skimmed over the pad beds in a rhythmic swinging motion, like that used in cutting hay with a scythe. I don't know how many strokes per minute a conditioned skitterer made, but a pickerel can move like chained lightning when he hears the dinner bell. Retrieving speed is the key to taking lunkers, and that applies to all methods of casting.

The skitter pole is ancient history now. Today you can do the same work with modern light tackle, get more fish, and have more fun in the process. And therein rests the case for chainsides. When approached without prejudice or heavy weapons, he's a first-class scrapper with a remarkable ability to live under the heels of civilization.

Clinic

When I was a very young boy, fishing for chain pickerel on the East Meadow Stream near Hempstead, Long Island, was a year-round passion. In the middle of winter with snow on the ground and ice on the water wherever the current didn't flow, I would cast a streamer fly from dawn until dusk. Pickerel are usually willing to cooperate, and I can't think of a more ideal species for a youngster starting his angling career. It's important to catch fish in the very beginning; otherwise interest flags, and the transcendental joys of angling aren't of much interest to children. Sunfish of any kind are a good substitute, and so are perch—but pickerel are bigger, and, when taken on very light spinning tackle, which any child can quickly master, this miniature pike is an inspiration. For that matter, the adult fly fisherman using weedless Keel-Hook bugs and streamer flies can spend many a happy hour catching pickerel.

Limited in distribution primarily to the eastern half of the United States but occurring as far west as the Navasota River in Texas, and in the Maritime Provinces of Canada to the north, chain pickerel have been recorded to 9 pounds, 6 ounces in Georgia, and 10 pounds, 4 ounces in Quebec. Other states that produce large fish are Maine, New Jersey, Virginia, and Florida.

INDEX

Chain pickerel (cont'd)
    techniques for, 273–74
    winter fishing for, 269, 275
Chalkstreams, European, 153–54,
    189, 219
Chappie, 69
Chapralis, Jim, 89–90
Chub Cay, 92
Clock, Phil, 79
Coachman Bucktail, 66
Columbia River, 106
Combs, Trey, 24
Connecticut River, 6–7, 226
Cook, Dr. William J., 49, 146
Cooper, Jack, 47
Coots, Abner, 256–58, 263
Coquille River, 105
Coronation, 69
Cortland, 82
Cortland hatchery, 29
Cosseboom, 228, 234
Cowdung, 176
Cowlitz River, 106
Crappie, 262
Cross, Reuben R., 154, 157
Cross Cay, 243
Cuda fly, 244
Cumming's Special, 101
Cunner, 247
Cushing, Fred, 88–89
Cutthroat trout, 28, 77, 186–87,
    194

Dace bucktail, 124
Dale Hollow, 56, 128
Damselflies, 60, 114–15, 124–25
Dark Buck Caddis, 140
Darning needles, 60, 114–15,
    124–25, 141, 272
Davis Strait, 208
de Lourdes Baiz, Dr. Miguel, 29
Dean River, 24–25
Deep Water Cay, 87, 96, 235,
    243
Deer Frog, 259, 266
Deerhair flies, 140–41
Delaware River, 23, 35, 56, 68,
    71, 73, 129, 179
    Big, 116, 121, 123, 126
    East Branch of, 58, 67, 126, 155
Deren, Jim, 132–33

Deschutes River, 100, 105–106,
    120
Deva Coapoacho Pool, 226
Devil Bugs, 259
Devil Mouse, 259
deZanger, Arie, 214–17, 221–22
Dieckman, Johnny, 48
Dilg, Will, 258–59
Dolomieu, 55
Donnelly, Roy, 69, 102, 141–42
Dorado, 47
Double turle knot, 83, 84–86
Doubs River, 218, 220
Drag, 181
Dragging fly, 181, 185, 187
Dragonflies, 60, 114–15, 124–25,
    141, 272
Drain, Wes, 102
Drake, Gilbert, 42, 235–36
Driva River, 203
Dropper strands, 41
Dry Fly and Fast Water, The
    (LaBranche), 1
Dyste, Mike, 14

East Meadow Stream, 275
East River, 247
Ecum Secum, 226
Edgartown, 255
Eel River, 28, 101, 104, 106
Eels, 45
Eisenhower, Dwight D., 247
Elitism, 231
Elliot, Bob, 60, 162
Esopus Creek, 23, 76, 121
Esquire, 214
Exman, Wally, 60, 62

Fanwing Royal Coachman, 4
Fast-water dry-fly fishing, 2–11
    air-resistant flies, 3–4
    casting techniques, 2, 5, 6–10
    drowned flies, 5
    hooks, 4, 5
    lair of fish, 6–7, 11
    leaders, 8–10
    light tackle, 2
    in pocket water, 6–8
    rods, 8
    spider-type flies, 4
    3-weight lines, 3